THE POLITICO'S GUIDE TO
POLITICS ON THE INTERNET

THE POLITICO'S GUIDE TO POLITICS ON THE INTERNET

by

Julian White

First published in Great Britain 1999
by Politico's Publishing
8 Artillery Row
London
SW1P 1RZ
United Kingdom
Tel: 0171 931 0090
Email: politicos@artillery-row.demon.co.uk
Web-site: http://www.politicos.co.uk

A catalogue record of this book is available from the British Library

ISBN 1902301331

Printed and bound in Great Britain by St. Edmundsbury Press
Cover Design by Ad Vantage

Julian White is the designer of the British Politics Home-page and the Politico's Website. He lives in Norfolk where he runs the web-site design company Aplex

Contents

This Directory

Every day British politics further embraces the internet revolution. The information super highway is here to stay and any politician who chooses to ignore it will surely be run over.

This directory introduces you to what has happened so far with the political situation on the Internet. It covers the good, the bad and the plain ugly of the political and politically related web-sites. At the end of this directory there is what I believe to be a complete and definitive list of British politics sites. If you know of any more that should be mentioned in future editions of this book, please send me an e-mail to julian@ukpol.co.uk.

Julian White
August 1999

Acknowledgements

For Richard Kimber and Brian Jarvis, for their help and support over the last few years, and for putting up with my obsession with politics and the Internet. Obsessions which, placed together, ended up creating the British Politics Page.

For all those people who helped me with the British Politics Page, including "abelard", Keith Edkins, Nigel Fletcher, Allan Foster, Stephen Hopkins, Stephen Horgan, Alex Macfie, Ian Ridley, Matt Robb, Colin Rosenstiel, Roy Stilling, Bruce Tober, and all those who I have inadvertently omitted.

For James McNulty, for taking over a work-load at Aplex whilst this directory was being produced, for helping with the production of the directory itself and for having the sheer nerve to start a business venture with me in the first place. Thanks also to Daniel Blakemore and Matthew Hardy of the Aplex Norwich Office for their help with the administration of the book.

Lastly, and most importantly, to my parents. For everything.

The Political On-Line Revolution:

As technological changes hit Westminster, we are seeing more and more institutions and political businesses going on-line. Just a few years ago it was difficult to believe that both Hansard and Houses of Parliament documentation would be available on-line, let alone all the information produced by Government departments, pressure groups, think-tanks, political parties and individuals. The wealth of political information available is becoming almost over-whelming in a very positive sense, and the growth is still continuing. The aim of this directory is to both show you round some of these sites, and also to keep a checklist of all the sites which are available for you to visit.

Back in the early 1990s, it seemed to be the Liberal Democrats who did the preparatory work with the Compuserve mailing lists and on-line discussion forums, which were supplemented shortly afterwards by Euan Bayliss' e-mail list. The Liberal Democrats were the first major political party to launch a web-site, shortly followed by the Labour Party, and followed after a long gap by the Conservative Party.

The Conservative Party web-site was set up in October 1995, run at the time by Web Works. Just in time for the Party Conference, the site had a variety of information sources and information on how to join the Party. The major complaint about the web-site was that you couldn't actually e-mail Conservative Central Office. A member of staff at the time said that this was simply because there were no resources to handle e-mail questions and suggestions in an effective manner. It took until just before the General Election for the Party to relent.

Constituency parties of all political persuasions frequently design their own sites, sometimes with great success, but sometimes with embarrassing consequences for the political parties they represent. Occasionally local party sites have been hacked into to the great displeasure of the Central Offices, such as the York Conservative Association in 1996.

Whilst the political parties were slowly coming on-line, some MPs started to develop their own web-sites. The former Conservative MP for Dover, David Shaw, started an early site, as did Ann Campbell, the Cambridge Labour MP. More and more MPs were going on-line and contactable by e-mail. In late 1996 the number was around 50, the number today is more than 100. There is far less excuse today. The Houses of Parliament are more accessible by e-mail for those MPs who wish to join the Internet revolution.

If you don't know your MP, you can always try guess-work. Some MPs do actually have e-mail addresses, although understandably they try and keep them relatively private so that they receive e-mails just from constituents, not from the whole world who wants to e-mail every MP that they can find. There is a trick. You need to know your MP's surname and initial, and simply put that into the address:

[surname][initial]@parliament.uk

So that if your MP was John Smith, try *SmithJ@parliament.uk*. It doesn't always work, but if your MP doesn't have an e-mail address that you know of, it can be worth a try. Failing that, ring the House of Commons and ask them!

In the early days of the Internet e-mail seemed a very direct way of contacting politicians. There were no problems with postage and it all seemed very immediate. Many people had visions of their elected representatives sitting by a computer preparing an answer to the question asked. Life is rarely like that. Today when an e-mail comes in, more often than not, it is printed out and dealt with in the same way as all other correspondence. As more people go on-line, e-mail may be a convenient way of contacting your MP, but don't get the impression it's more direct. It rarely is. And one note of caution, don't 'spam' an e-mail to every MP's e-mail address you can in order to further your cause. It will only be deleted, and all you will do is play your part in deterring more

MPs from getting e-mail addresses, which is still an important target to aim for!

Government departments themselves have often been more forthcoming about going on-line, with the Government's official server starting in the early 1990s. The departments have always had a range of information, and press releases available to anyone who wanted them. Although some Government Departments remain better than others in terms of quality, and there are details of all the larger Departments in this directory, they have all understood the need to make available information about how they work, how to contact them, and provide lists of publications and press releases which they produce.

In 1996, 10 Downing Street itself went on-line, with a tour of the famous house, and information about past Prime Ministers. Even the Monarchy, that most traditional of institutions, decided to launch a web-site, and it remains one of the better Internet sites of any type around. This was nothing compared to the arrival of the newspapers, such as the Times and the Telegraph, on-line which themselves provided a large amount of searchable information and with back issues. All for free. This meant that the Internet user was able to find out political news over the previous year and this enabled many people to learn more about what was happening in the world of current affairs.

But the most important development was the arrival of Hansard on-line. For the first time you didn't have to have an expensive subscription to Hansard, you could access what our elected representatives in the House of Commons and our not so elected representatives in the House of Lords were saying. To those interested in politics, this was an amazing resource. Debates were on-line within just a few hours. From being a luxury, the Internet now became an essential tool for anyone wanting a cheap and effective solution to finding out more about politics.

There is still a long way to go, however, and there is a lot more information that could be placed on-line. Government departments can always provide more information, and more councils need to follow the lead of forward-looking councils such as Hampshire, in developing an informative and substantial web-site that local people will access to find out more about their area, and their local politics. We will know when we have nearly made it, however, and that is when we finally see the vast majority of MPs using e-mail, and being contactable by e-mail readily and easily.

A resource which many thought was expensive to start off with, with high ISP charges and expensive phone bills, has now turned into a very affordable and effective way to find out more about politics and politicians. More and more companies now offer free phone calls to the Internet and others offer free connection to their services. Some politicians don't like it, and some said it would never happen, but the Internet is about to play a crucial part in British democracy.

There has been great progress with both the development of the Internet in the UK and of the development of politically related websites. But given all the information which is now available to us across all the different institutions and groups, what can we expect in the future?

The Houses of Parliament are now "wired-up", with all of our elected representatives having access to e-mail. As time progresses it seems that we also need more and more of the Councillors in this country on-line, and various different local authorities are now starting to supply, and publicise, e-mail addresses for both their Councillors, and for their own staff.

The future of web-sites is likely to see more and more information and archives provided by the larger institutions, and certainly for the short-term, access to this will be free. As time progresses the people will probably start to demand more and more access to Government information on-line, and some of the Government departments where progress has been slow are likely to catch up. Such events will hopefully also improve accountability.

A lot of the sites in this directory have long lists of publications which they produce. Some have gone to the extreme of putting all the text of all the documents on for free, some have produced the text free for members only, some have produced short extracts of each publication before letting you buy the hard copy, and some list them by title only. The trend however is towards putting more and more information on the Internet for free. It attracts readers, and a bigger readership gives the institution more credibility and opportunity to have their case listened to, their product sold, or whatever else their aim is.

The Internet, so some said, was going to end the printed publication. We were going to see books replaced by disks and on-line publishing. Instead, the technology of the Internet has aided the development of the book, as books are sold on-line, and buyers are able to read book reviews and find out more about books than they could previously, all at the touch of a button (or maybe at the touch of a few buttons).

Local Government needs to understand the on-line revolution in exactly the same way as the national Government. Only the United States beats the United Kingdom for the sheer amount of political information and institutions which have gone on-line. Local Government has, in parts, met this challenge, and this directory contains sites which are truly excellent examples of how local authorities can perform. The day when we can e-mail any councillor or any council worker about any problem is the day that we have more power to demand better local services.

People often don't consider the development of local Government web-sites as being all that important, even though the same principle of empowerment still applies. If a street light doesn't work, many people won't go to the effort of working out who to contact, and then go to the effort of informing them. With some councils, you can already send this information on-line. In a few years this should be common-place. In short, this means that individuals can easily inform their local authorities of matters they want resolving. If more and more people do this, it means that local government must become even more responsive to peoples' needs, and it shows that the Internet can have a positive effect on all levels of Government.

More information is on-line than ever before and it is more easily accessible. The Internet has shown us that, for the moment at least, it is the gateway to a more open democracy.

In the next section in this directory, you will find a large number of web-sites. Some are the best of their kind, some are full of information, some are full of promise, some are long overdue, and some are plain ugly. This part isn't meant to be totally definitive. For such a list, please use the large index of all sites in the back of the directory.

The best web-sites in their chosen categories are mentioned, and although this is inevitably largely subjective, all comments are welcomed. You will find at the back of this directory a list of the top ten web-sites on the Internet, and suggestions for promotion (or indeed relegation) from this list will be gratefully received.

For now, happy exploring!

Books

BOOK REVIEWS:

British Politics Page
http://www.ukpol.co.uk/books.htm

This site contains reviews of around fifty books, from books about particular political parties to biographies of politicians. The site is regularly updated to feature new books and the reviews are written by numerous volunteers to provide a wider scope of opinions. It is also useful to those doing political courses about British politics who want to know which textbooks are the best ones for them to purchase.

BOOKSTORES:

Politico's Book-Store
http://www.politicos.co.uk/

Politico's is a unique London bookstore, which sells just about anything you could think of related to British politics. They have a wide range of books, both new and old, and you can find a large number of best-sellers and subject listings, with the opportunity to order a catalogue on-line. In addition to their stock of new and used books, you can also find a coffee-house at their London store, as well as items such as signed letters by politicians, political collectables and even political underwear.

LIBRARIES:

British Library
http://portico.bl.uk/

The British Library in central London is the biggest in the country. On the web-site, you are able to search OPAC for the list of books in stock, and there are also details of how you can visit the library, how to retrieve books and useful links to other book related resources around the world. A number of the printed fact-sheets have also been made available on-line.

If you do need to find a political book for research, then visiting the university library sites would be a good start. You will find that nearly all have their entire stock available for searching on-line, and you can then arrange to either visit that library or gain an intra-library loan for your research. You can find a list of these at *http://www.bubl.ac.uk/link/a/academiclibrariesinengland.htm*, as well as other libraries throughout the world.

PUBLISHERS:

Carlton Publishing Group
http://www.carlton-group.co.uk/

Carlton publish a range of different books on Government and Whitehall, and they have included often quite detailed indexes of what is in these books on their web-site. It's a nicely presented site but it would be nice if they could re-produce on-line some of the contents of their publications which would be of genuine use to the Internet user.

Politico's Publishing
http://www.politicos.co.uk/publ.htm

Politico's Publishing publish a range of books relating to politics and elections. This site has details of those books and further information on how to order them. Topics include the Jeremy Thorpe memoirs to the collected speeches of Ann Widdecombe. This publishing company is an off-shoot of a political book-store set-up in London just two years ago, which now fills a growing niche market.

Here are some other political publishers (Also see the think tanks section):

Ashgate
http://www.ashgate.com

Blackwell Publishers
http://blackwellpublishers.co.uk

Frank Cass
http://frankcass.com

Debrett's Peerage
http://debretts.co.uk

Edinburgh University Press
http://www.eup.ed.ac.uk

Faber & Faber
http://www.faber.co.uk

Friends of the Earth
http://www.foe.co.uk

HarperCollins
http://fireandwater.com

Harvard University Press
http://www.hup.harvard.edu

Hodder & Stoughton
http://u-net.com/hodder/

Lawrence & Wishart
http://l-w-bks.co.uk

Macmillan
http://macmillan.co.uk

Manchester University Press
http://www.man.ac.uk/mup

Open University Press
http://bookshop.cp.uk/openup/

Oxford University Press
http://oup.co.uk

Penguin
http://penguin.com

Pluto Press
www.leevalley.co.uk/plutopress

Random House
http://www.randomhouse.com

Routledge
http://www.routledge.com/routledge.html

Joseph Rowntree Foundation
http://jrf.org.uk

Sage Publications
http://www.sagepub.co.uk

The Stationery Office
http://www.the-stationery-office.co.uk

Verso
http://www.verso-nir.com

The Women's Press
http://www.the-womens-press.com

Yale University Press
http://www.yale.edu/yup

* * *

There aren't many web-sites which have been set-up about one specific book, but one of interest at the moment, although actually American, might be useful for some budding British politicians. It's titled "How To Win a High School Election" and can be seen at *http://www.schoolelection.com/*. Here you can find free excerpts on how you can make yourself popular enough to be elected to a position of authority even if you're not a particularly interesting or well-liked person. Without mentioning names, such tactics could be useful to a number of British politicians.

Councils

If this directory had been written about two or three years ago, you would probably have been able to see every single council site that existed featured in this section of the directory. The growth in size and number of local authority web-sites since then has been amazing, with the vast majority of councils now on-line. It is expected that nearly every other large authority will be on-line within the next two years, and then we expect more and more of the town and parish councils in the country to start developing web-sites.

There has also been an important change in emphasis in the content of local authority sites. I feel that council sites should not just be tourist brochures for their local area, but that they should be resources for local people to find out more about how their council works. Sites like Aberdeenshire Council, *http://www.aberdeenshire.gov.uk/,* are very colourful, but other than mentioning in passing which political party is in control of the council, there is no more information about the council or how it runs.

It is easy to forget that when someone has a problem, they don't know who they can call on to help. If a council web-site can provide that information, as well as lists of Councillors and dates and times of council meetings, then it is genuinely useful as an informational site. Angus Council's web-site, if you can get around the strange navigation system, at *http://www.angus.gov.uk/,* has a comprehensive map and Councillor information within the site.

Then there are some sites which are truly magnificent resources for their local community, such as the Birmingham City Council web-site at *http://www.birmingham.gov.uk/.* There is an interesting feature where you can report a problem with anything from a grit bin being damaged to a pot hole in a road through to a missing sign-post. This is in addition to all the council and councillor's information. One wonders why they can't all be like this.

Councils should be warned though, although no names will be mentioned in this case, to save the embarrassment of this South coast council, but a member of one council's IT department thought he would use the council web-space to sell his own computer chips, chips which happened to let you run copied Playstation games.

There is an interesting observation behind this, which is that the Councillors in many of these towns don't see and often don't have much interest in the web-sites. They are usually lovingly created by an IT department without much thought from the Councillors about what information local people would find interesting, and often without much accountability about what goes on-line. The future for all council web-sites is that they should be truly useful resources for the local population, where you can ask questions and get in touch with paid council officials, as well as Councillors, with any problems you might have. That might even lead to easing the problem with voter apathy in local elections that we see today.

Another slightly alarming feature of some web-sites, Torbay (*http://www.torbay.gov.uk/*) for example, is the attempt to sell off space on the council site to businesses and charging to local businesses for being included in a web directory. This practice is slightly disappointing given that council sites should be focusing on providing impartial and free information to the public, not concentrating on making money from businesses and providing links only to those who pay extra money.

The Local Government Association at *http://www.lga.gov.uk/* is a body which was launched on the 1st April 1997 to represent local authorities in England and Wales. The pages are slightly out-of-date in places, but members can access a large range of documents relating to local Government as well as the LGA's events and policies.

One of the official sites for local Government is run by the Department for Transport, Environment and the Regions (DETR), and can be found at *http://www.local.detr.gov.uk/.* Information on this website is of interest to both the casual reader, and to users looking for specific information. In common with most Government sites, you can find the department's press releases and certain documents related to local

Government. Additionally there are a range of guides, such as for council tax, which can be found at *http://www.local.doe.gov.uk/finance/ctax/-ctax.htm*.

There is another site available with further information about local Government, at *http://www.local.gov.uk/*. The site is relatively short on detailed information, but it gives a range of "help-sheet" type pages on what the procedures of local Government are and how they should be followed, and it gives advice on what rights you have to have access to your councillor and to access official council information.

On the DETR's web-site you can also find an interesting history of local government at *http://www.local.doe.gov.uk/struct/history.htm*, which gives details of how the structure works. Despite the existence of a range of official sites and local government bodies, it has been left to an individual to produce one of the most comprehensive pages with links to all of the local council web-sites.

Keeping up-to-date with the growing number of council web-sites is always difficult, especially given the recent expansion in numbers. However, Charles Sale has set up his own immensely valuable site which lists all the local councils, not just in the UK, but also around the world. He set the site up after looking at a large number of other council web-sites and finding that they often "contained lots of bad links, no indication of where particular councils were located or no indication of what type of council they were." The site Charles Sale created at *http://www.oultwood.com/localgov/index.htm* is now a very popular one which receives a lot of positive feedback, and he hopes that he has produced "a reference tool which would help users to not only find council web sites in a particular area but also find out more about the structure of local government in a variety of countries". I tend to agree, and the site has been awarded fifth place in this directory's top ten web-sites.

One interesting observation he has made about the site is that he gets a 400% increase in access numbers when local elections are being held. This gives additional credence to the view that people want to see election results, and that councils should make a priority of displaying them on their sites. The Internet is one of the easiest ways for people to find election results in their local areas, and hopefully councils will recognise that they should be contributing to this.

On Handy's page, at *http://www.oultwood.com/localgov/linksites.htm* you can find a list of those councils which have useful links pages to other external sites of interest. More usefully, he also lists all those councils who do not yet have web-sites, and although the number is falling, there are still quite a lot of councils with work to do. You can find this "shame list" at *http://www.oultwood.com/localgov/nowebsite.htm*.

Inevitably, this page on Handy's site will get shorter and shorter, and it isn't overly crass to say that local democracy will be the winner as all the councils get themselves on-line and councillors and council workers find themselves easier to contact than ever before.

Political Resources on the Internet

A long time ago it wasn't very easy to find out what political resources there actually were on the Internet, which is why I decided to start up the British Politics Page, which is available at *http://www.ukpol.co.uk/*. Also listed below are the other directories which people have compiled about politics and similar subjects, and how to work the official Government Directory to get the most out of it. All these directories have been compiled by individuals without funding for their sites, so be forgiving if some of them aren't totally complete or haven't been updated recently.

There are a large number of on-line resources which feature past election results. Although no institutional site possesses a large on-line archive, you often find that the newspaper sites such as the Times and The Telegraph feature comprehensive coverage of large elections as and when they take place. Often you can get information about results from the archives of these papers, or you can try the useful resources below, which are all run by volunteers.

GENERAL POLITICAL RESOURCES:

British Politics Page
http://www.ukpol.co.uk/

I started this set of web-pages was in 1995 to supply information about British Politics and Elections on the Internet, and to link together all the that currently exist on-line about British Politics. If information was already available, I took the policy of just linking to it, and if that information was not available, I tried to make that information available. The site has undergone many restructures to contain the vast array of information that it does today, and remains one of the largest non-institutional sites of its kind around. On the site you can find links to thousands of other political sites on the Internet, book reviews, election results, political and electoral news, and much more.

Ivor Peska's Web-Page
http://www.club.demon.co.uk/

This on-line resource was started by Ivor when he was at Warwick University, and was a frequent poster to the uk.politics. news-groups. The resource has a host of election results available, and links to other sites of interest. One of the most useful features of this interesting site are maps which show the state of the parties after the May local election which are held every year. You can also see maps of the country, showing each party's strength by colour, at each General Election since 1983, with each map becoming progressively less and less blue. You can see the map at: *http://www.club.demon.co.uk/Politics/Maps/map-now.gif.*

David Boothroyd's Election Page
http://www.election.demon.co.uk/

David Boothroyd knows nearly everything about elections, and this site contains hundreds of election results going back to 1983. The site also has information by constituency, but the General Election results are the most useful feature, and a superb reference guide for those interested in psephology. Also on Boothroyd's site, you can find a host of other information, ranging from the times and order of constituency declarations in 1997 (Sunderland South declared first, Winchester was last), to a list of all seats which have changed hands since 1974. These pages can be found at *http://www.election.demon.co.uk/declar.html.* and *http://www.election.demon.co.uk/changes.html* respectively.

There are many more pages like this to explore through on this site, and some of the information stored here isn't available anywhere else on the Internet. Should you wish to find very recent election results, David Boothroyd is also a regular poster to the uk.politics. news-groups, find a host of new data being posted there with

s on the Net
n.it/politic/uk.htm

s has links to political and electoral sites in numer-
is also an interesting election page available from
w.agora.stm.it/elections/election/unking.htm.

esources
ac.uk/

hard Kimber, covers politics world-wide and has a
tical sites of various kinds. It also contains sections
al thought, political theory, and a range of other
f you require a site which covers nearly every coun-
starting point for anything political or electoral, this
al political sites.

* * *

elections, and so the number of sites featuring the
ropean, local and Northern Ireland local elections
antially, with new sites being made available every

RESOURCES:

ges
lk/

ay be slightly biased to the nationalists, but they
g and useful set of resources about Scottish poli-
y the best first stop for anyone who wants electoral
the country. There is a range of election results and
which has always been kept up-to-date and timely.
n Old says that "I initially set it up as there were

many questions about election and referendum results on Scottish political discussion groups and mailing lists and at that point there was almost nothing about Scottish Politics on the web. I found that setting up a web site where the data was freely accessible was easier than looking up files and posting the information every time. So, I set up the site on 25th March 1996."

Old also prepared an immensely useful set of web-pages about Scottish politics before the 1997 General Election, including profiles of every constituency, this will hopefully be repeated before the next General Election.

GENERAL ELECTION RESULTS

Three sites in the previous section contain a host of General Election results. The British Politics Page, at *http://www.ukpol.co.uk/profile.htm* has the results of the 1997 General Election, whilst David Boothroyd's site contains results back to 1983.

EUROPEAN ELECTION RESULTS

The European election results for 1999 can be found at *http://www.whirlwind.co.uk/* along with the Scottish Parliament and Welsh Assembly votes. Past European election results are not yet fully available on the Internet, with the exception of the 1994 European Election results, which are archived on the David Boothroyd site at *http://www.election.demon.co.uk/ep1994.html.*

LOCAL ELECTION RESULTS:

Local election results are posted every week by Colin Rosenstiel, a Cambridge Councillor, to the political newsgroup uk.politics.electoral, and these are archived at *http://www.ukpol.co.uk/coun.htm* every month. The Conservatives often use these figures to prove how well they're doing, and Keith Edkins who is also from Cambridge, runs an analysis over the figures so that you can see exactly how each party is doing.

Also on the British Politics Page, and on Ivor Peksa's page (*http://www.club.demon.co.uk/*), you will find the results of the local elections which are held every May. These area by area results provide an interesting comparison of each party's electoral fortunes as the years progress. As yet though, no site on the Internet contains a comprehensive list of all results, as the producers of these sites are usually reliant on posters to the political news-groups for their information.

SUMMARY ELECTION RESULTS:

Summary results of each General Election result are held at *http://www.ukpol.co.uk/table.htm*, where you can see the percentage of votes attained by each party since 1945, as well as a list of every Cabinet Minister since 1945. You can also find a list of all the Prime Ministers since 1800 linked from this site. So if you do ever need to know who the Defence Secretary in 1963 happened to be, you now know where to find the answer! Well, some of us wake up in the night wanting to know such things.

Government Department Web-Sites

Despite co-operation between Government Departments the quality of the different web-sites varies immensely. Some of the sites are infrequently updated and need a lot of work to make them a useful resource to the public, whilst others shine with their information, design and speed. The Government Web Server was set up in 1994 to enable all of the Government departments to grow around a common theme.

Specifically, for each major Government department, you will find the department's main web-page at the top, then followed (if applicable) by pages which deal with Ministerial information, press releases, responsibilities of the department, speeches made by the Ministers, and the spending plans of the department.

It was under the Major administration that Government departments started to go on-line, and more and more information slowly became available. Department press releases were one of the first chunks of information to go on-line, and were very useful at the time for understanding the scope and relevance of each department.

As mentioned elsewhere the development of Hansard was one of the major advances in the political on-line revolution. Hansard was otherwise a very expensive publication, it costs more than £1,000 a year to subscribe to both the House of Lords and House of Commons printed versions of Hansard. In general, only large public libraries and university libraries stock the journal as few members of the public can afford buy it for themselves (although the young William Hague did as a schoolboy). For this to go on-line meant that an archive was available to see what politicians were saying, and small as it may seem now, this was a major advance for democracy.

Department of Agriculture, Fisheries and Food

Department web page: *http://www.maff.gov.uk/*
Ministerial information: *http://www.maff.gov.uk/aboutmaf/*
Responsibilities: *http://www.maff.gov.uk/aboutmaf/deprep/cover.htm*
Speeches: *http://www.maff.gov.uk/aboutmaf/minspech/default.htm*

The Ministry of Agriculture, Fisheries and Food's Minister is the Rt. Hon. Nick Brown (*http://www.maff.gov.uk/nbrown.htm*). This site is divided into farming, environment, fisheries and food representing the wide work of the department. Although the site is quite low on graphics, it is presented in a manner which makes information relatively easy to find, although an overview to the department might be a useful addition. The site's lack of heavy graphics also speeds up the general accessing of the pages.

There is a useful statistics section included on the site and also a good section on BSE which gives a range of information, including a glossary to try and decipher the rather scientific language which is used on this section of the site. An agency set up in response to the BSE crisis is the Meat Hygiene Service they can be found at *http://www.maff.gov.uk/aboutmaf/agency/mhs.htm*, and there is further information at *http://www.bse.org.uk/*.

Also on the site is information about the Farming and Rural Conservation Agency, an agency set up to focus on local issues, farming and conservation. This site is similar to the department's site generally, not graphically intensive, but simply and plainly presented with the information readily available.

Although most of the department's publications are listed, most are not available on-line, even those which are free to order from the department. Given the time it would take to make some of these documents available, their omission is something which will hopefully be rectified in the future. Like a number of other departments, MAFF has details of how to obtain a range of other information from the department and the charges for providing that information.

A useful section within the 'About MAFF' pages is a list of contact details for each section of the department. Not all Government departments have this information, and it makes contacting the right people simpler for all concerned. Although the vast majority of these sections cannot be accessed directly by e-mail, there are a range of contact e-mail addresses around the site for ordering department publications, commenting on the design to the site and making suggestions for additional content to the site.

Some sections of the site have become outdated, including the coastal defence pages which detail the department's policy towards funding projects to stop coastal erosion in important areas. The page hasn't been updated since mid-1996 and the information has become outdated since.

Department of Culture, Media and Sport
Department web page: *http://www.culture.gov.uk/*
Ministerial information: *None available*
Press releases: *http://www.coi.gov.uk/coi/depts/GHE/GHE.html*
Responsibilities: *http://www.culture.gov.uk/corpinfo.htm*
Speeches: *None available*

This department, currently run by Chris Smith, used to be known as the Ministry of Fun. The web-site, first set up in May 1997, is short on a lot of the information that the other Government departments supply, with little details about the Ministerial team, the speeches or the responsibilities of the Department. There are however e-mail addresses for each of the Ministerial team, something which it would be nice to see repeated for all Government Ministers.

There is a section of the web-site about the National Lottery at *http://www.lottery.culture.gov.uk/*, which provides detailed information on how the lottery operates and how local communities can apply for lottery grants. Details about the Millennium Commission can be found at *http://www.millennium.gov.uk/*.

Another site operated by the Department gives everyone an opportunity to comment on the department's proposals to build a commemorative garden for Diana, Princess of Wales in Kensington Garden. Anyone can cast their on-line opinion at *http://www.dianagarden.org.uk/*.

The site itself occasionally contains dates of important events, but this is neither comprehensive enough or entirely up-to-date. An alternative site to find such information can be found at the Tourist Authority's site at *http://www.visitbritain.com/*.

Overall, there simply isn't enough information on this web-site to make it a very useful resource, which is especially disappointing since one of the department's responsibilities is the promotion of new media. Many of the documents which are available on the site are only available in .pdf format, when they would have been more accessible by making them available in standard html format.

There are places on the site which mention that lots of further information will be added soon, so this slightly under-stated web-site may gradually become a more informative and complete web-site than it currently is.

Ministry of Defence
Department web page: *http://www.mod.uk/*
Ministerial information: *http://www.mod.uk/sofs.htm*
Press releases: *http://www.mod.uk/new/news.htm*
Responsibilities: *http://www.mod.uk/aboutmod/*
Speeches: *http://www.mod.uk/other.htm*

The Ministry of Defence has a wide range of information on its site. The site is well-presented and remains attractive, without using excessive graphics. There is a large amount of information provided about the Ministerial team, with their biographies and their responsibilities.

There is a useful section for those businesses who wish to supply the Ministry of Defence, and they are given their own section at *http://www.mod.uk/commercial/commercial.htm*. There is a range of information pages on how individual companies can sell products and services to the armed forces.

Each of the armed forces are given their own web-site, the Royal Navy have a very graphics intensive site at *http://www.royal navy.mod.uk/*, the British Army have a very interesting and smooth site at *http://www.army.mod.uk/*, and the Royal Air Force have a simple but useful site at *http://www.raf.mod.uk/*. Should you be tempted to join the British Army, you can choose to take the on-line challenge first at *http://www.army.mod.uk/army/challeng/index.htm* which lets you see if you are able to make sensible and effective military decisions. The Territorials also have a site at *http://www.army.mod.uk/army/organise/ta/main.htm*.

The Ministry of Defence's web-site has a large amount of detail regarding the policies of the department. An example is the Strategic Defence Review at *http://www.mod.uk/policy/sdr/index.htm*, where comprehensive information about the review is included on-line. This commitment to open information is also seen in a series of pages at *http://www.mod.uk/policy/gulfwar/index.htm* which give information and statistical resources about illnesses faced by Gulf Veterans.

A section of the site at *http://www.dstan.mod.uk/home.htm*, contains details about the Defence Standards Body which has a review and the latest details of the work done in maintaining defence standards. A nice addition which backs all these sections is an archive at *http://www.mod.uk/archive/archive.htm*, which includes a range of graphics which can be used, such as the Ministry of Defence crest and logo.

For more information about defence policy, you can also visit NATO's web-site at *http://www.nato.int/* which has copious details about the organisation and its policies. At the time of writing there was also a special 50th anniversary section with details about the organisation in the last half century.

Department of Education and Employment
Department web page: *http://www.dfee.gov.uk/*
Ministerial information: *http://www.dfee.gov.uk/miniresp.htm*
Press releases: *http://www.dfee.gov.uk/news/press.htm*
Spending plans: *http://www.dfee.gov.uk/news/53.htm*

The Department of Education and the Department of Employment were merged together in 1995, with Gillian Shepherd taking over the new, department. After the 1997 General Election, David Blunkett became the Secretary of State for Education and Employment. This web-site, which for a long time was housed in a hard to find sub-directory of the Government server, provides a wide range of information about the various training and employment schemes which are available to people.

The web-site has recently been re-designed, although judging from the new look, not for the better. The navigation of the site has also been made unnecessarily cumbersome. Underneath the very clunky set of front-pages is a very useful set of web-pages with a large amount of information which has been placed on-line. There are very complete details of the responsibilities of each Minister, although no biographies have been included on the site, nor any contact details.

As with other Government department sites, there are comprehensive lists of which publications are available, but very few of them have been made available on-line. In terms of cost-effectiveness, it doesn't appear sensible to send out free documents on request by post rather than simply putting them into HTML format. It is likely that more documents will however be made available over the coming months and years as demand increases.

The Education Standards Site can be visited at *http://www.standards.dfee.gov.uk/*, which contains information on good teaching practices and the site aims to become a useful resources for students and parents in monitoring and maintaining high education standards. The National Curriculum has its own site at *http://www.dfee.gov.uk/nc/* with a summary of the curriculum, and details of how to obtain copies.

One of Labour's key pledges before the 1997 General Election was to deliver on youth unemployment. Part of their plan to do that was through the New Deal, and a very nice set of pages (albeit in a very orange colour) are available at *http://www.newdeal.gov.uk/*. The site answers questions which are most often asked, and it would be nice to see such a simple feature on more sites generally. A special mention should be made for the New Deal site, as the pages on this site are available in many different languages, and even a large text version. Both of these ideas are very rare on web-sites at the moment. Although the language of the Internet may be English, it is nice to see departments and agencies making an effort to ensure documents are as accessible as possible.

Overall, because of the very large coverage of the department, there is a wealth of information available on the site, although it is not always easy to find what you are looking for.

Department of the Environment, Transport and the Regions
Department web page: *http://www.detr.gov.uk/*
Ministerial information: *http://www.detr.gov.uk/thisis/4.htm*
Press releases: *http://www.nds.coi.gov.uk/coi/coipress.htm*
Responsibilities: *http://www.detr.gov.uk/thisis/detr.htm*
Speeches: *http://www.detr.gov.uk/pubs/index.htm*

The Department of the Environment, Transport and the Regions is John Prescott's (*http://www.detr.gov.uk/thisis/prescott.htm*) domain. John Prescott is also Deputy Prime Minister, so this department's profile has been raised considerably since it was formerly the Departments of the Environment and Transport.

The web-site is very comprehensive, detailing the role of this new department. The department is also responsible for local Government, and there are a range of resources on housing. The front-page is one of the most graphically pleasing, as well as being fast to load, of any political web-site I have seen.

The department is responsible for environmental matters, and there is a useful section on the site called the UK Environment in Facts and Figures at *http://www.environment.detr.gov.uk/epsim/index.htm*, which contains details of a large range of environmental statistics. Another useful part of the site is dedicated to drinking water quality, and there are reports on the quality of the water which we drink, as well as information on the water in the sea, and the levels of pollution in each area. Further information about the water industry is available at *http://www.dwi.detr.gov.uk/h2oinfo.htm.*

The Department is responsible for public transport, and the infamous integrated transport policy. There is information on the department's public transport policies and aims at *http://www.local-transport.detr .gov.uk/.* There are also links from the site to the DVLA (Driver and Vehicle Licensing Authority) site at *http://www.open.gov.uk/dvla,* which has details of how to get a driving license and how to keep your vehicle legally registered.

A problem that has been seen in the past with this department is that a large amount of information about the work of the department has only been available by purchasing hard copies of documents. It seems that recently more documents are being made available on-line, and hopefully this positive trend will continue. Praise should also go to this site for making the department accessible to everyone, with the inclusion of literally hundreds of e-mail addresses to different members of the Department. E-mail addresses are provided not just for different parts of the Department, but also for the Ministerial team.

The department is an enormous one which sprawls across many areas of Government, from transport, the environment, local Government, and many other areas, but this site does well to make so much information available so well.

Department of Health
Department Web-page: http://www.doh.gov.uk/
Minister Information: http://www.doh.gov.uk/minister/minister.htm
Press Release: http://www.coi.gov.uk/depts/GDH/BDH.html
Responsibilities: http://www.doh.gov.uk/about.htm

The Department of Health is currently run by Frank Dobson, and information on both the Secretay of State and the Department's Ministers can be found at *http://www.doh.gov.uk/minister/minister.htm*. The site is relatively comprehensive, although it not a very colourful site with only minimal use being made of graphics. The advantage of this is that the site is relatively fast to load, and it is generally easy to find the information you require.

There are a large range of information documents available on the site, most of which are stored in .pdf format. These cover everything from what the department does, to the department annual review and information pack. There is a section entitled POINT, which has details of the department's publications with links to the on-line versions where available. This can be seen at *http://www.doh.gov.uk/pointh.htm*.

The department's site has information about general health-care issues, and when the latest food scare raises its head, the department usually has at least a set of press releases available, or sometimes entire sections of its web-site, in a bid to provide as much information as possible to the public about the scare.

The Health Education Authority has its own site at *http://www. hea.org.uk/*, which has details of health campaigns which it has run, from alcohol to cancer, as well as details of what the Authority does, and how it is run. The well-designed site has a number of databases which can be searched for further information, and there are numerous links to other sites which are of interest.

The NHS was 50 years old in 1998, and a special web-site set up to cover this provided interesting information about the department, and statistics about how the service was run. This is available from *http://www.nhs50.nhs.uk/*. Although there are over 400 pages of information the site may not be available in early 2000, but there is useful information currently being provided on the site.

For those patients who like league tables and similar items, there are a host of information tables, again in .pdf format, which cover the performance of each Trust in every area, under a whole range of different criteria. The information is available in a number of formats, so you can even get the data in a format that can be used straight in your spreadsheet. The information is updated on a regular basis, and provides a useful guide to how hospitals are doing.

The Home Office

Department web page: *http://www.homeoffice.gov.uk/*
Ministerial info: *http://www.homeoffice.gov.uk/ministers/ho_mints.htm*
Press releases: *http://www.nds.coi.gov.uk/coi/coipress.nsf*
Responsibilities: *http://www.homeoffice.gov.uk/dob/index.htm*

The Home Office covers a very wide range of responsibilities, and the web-site for this department offers a very good basis for understanding the wide scope which is on offer. A substantial amount of documents are available on-line, however this is another department which possibly relies too heavily on the usage of .pdf documents which can be cumbersome to read and tedious to down-load. Most of the documentation is laid out in a logical and easy-to-find manner.

On this site you can find a link to the Public Appointments Unit, *http://www.open.gov.uk/pau/pauhome.htm*, which gives details of appointments to non-Governmental bodies and NHS Trusts. Details are available for a wide range of Departments, not just the Home Office. The pages also give details of who exactly has been appointed to the various public positions, how long their period of office lasts and how much they earn each year from the appointment.

The web-site is split into smaller parts, each covering a section of the department's work. The Prison Service web-site can be found at *http://www.hmprisonservice.gov.uk/*, which is a very nicely presented site, although much of the information is currently not available. A very plain, but still functional, set of pages are available for the UK Passport Agency at *http://www.open.gov.uk/ukpass/ukpass.htm*.

The Home Office has a relatively large number of agencies and non-governmental organisations which support the department, and a section of the Home Office site at http://www.homeoffice.gov.uk/agency.htm links to these various bodies agencies include the Commission for Racial Equality (*http://www.open.gov.uk/cre/crehome.htm*) and the National Criminal Intelligence Service (*http://www.open.gov.uk/ncis/ncis home.htm*), amongst others.

Details about the police are on the site at *http://www.homeoffice. gov.uk/pstc.htm*, which features a general guide to the police and a number of ways for individuals to tackle crime themselves. Information about the various police forces in the country, including links to those forces who have their own web-sites, can be found at *http://www.police.uk/*. Two of the more well-known forces with web-sites are the Metropolitan Police (*http://www.met.police.uk/*) and the Northern Ireland's Royal Ulster Constabulary (*http://www.ruc.police.uk/*).

The Foreign and Commonwealth Office
Department web page: *http://www.fco.gov.uk/*
Ministerial info: *http://www.fco.gov.uk/directory/dynpage.asp?Page=14*
Press releases: *None available*
Responsibilities: *None available*
Speeches: *http://www.fco.gov.uk/news/speech.asp*
Spending plans: *None available*

Surprisingly for such a traditional department, the Foreign Office was one of the first Government departments to launch its own web-site, and it has remained probably the best departmental web-site in terms of both content and presentation. Indeed, it wins this directory's award for the best departmental web-site, and remains the web-site that other Government departments should try to match.

A wide range of information is available on the site, from Ministers' speeches, information on foreign countries, relevant news for travellers, and other similar advice. The speeches section at *http://www.fco. gov.uk/news/speech.asp* is especially good, with a large number of speeches which are all nicely and compactly displayed.

The travel advice section is very detailed, and the pages remain a useful source of information for those people who are overseas. The pages at *http://www.fco.gov.uk/travel/default.asp* give advice as to which countries to avoid, and what precautions to take when visiting certain other countries. The information provided for every country is very detailed, ranging from what precautions to take against crime to what medical precautions to take.

There is a very comprehensive news section available covering many different countries around the world, and information is made available very promptly on-line. This is in contrast to some of the other Government departments, where it can take days for the latest news or events to be reflected on the web-site.

A section of the web-site gives information on how British companies can trade abroad, and what Government partnerships are available to help with this. This is available at *http://www.fco.gov.uk/trade/*, and provides valuable resources to any business which exports.

The Foreign Office site is a very comprehensive affair, which can be trusted to make available information in a timely and effective manner. For those users who choose to register, which is without charge, you can get parts of the site personalised so that you can find information of relevance to you even quicker.

If only all Government sites were like this........

Department of Trade and Industry
Department web page: *http://www.dti.gov.uk/*
Ministerial information: *http://www.dti.gov.uk/Ministers.html*
Press releases: *http://www.nds.coi.gov.uk/*
Responsibilities: *http://www.dti.gov.uk/public/aboutdti.html*
Speeches: *http://www.dti.gov.uk/public/news.html*

This web-site is quite an informative one, although it is one of the decreasing number of Government departments to still use frames, and this sometimes detracts from the look of the pages. You can also access the site at *http://www2.dti.gov.uk/* should the index page listed above not be available. However the site is otherwise smartly designed, and finding the information required is usually an effortless task.

If you want to supply products or services to the Department, then you can find information on how to tender and get more information generally from *http://www.dti.gov.uk/about/suppliers/foreword.htm*. Given all that they say about prompt payment to small business, it is nice to see their commitment towards paying their own bills within 30 days, *http://www.dti.gov.uk/about/suppliers/payment.htm*.

There is a section on science and industry which contains details of a range of different initiatives. One of these is Foresight, which aims to "develop visions of the future", and which can be found at *http://www.foresight.gov.uk/*. Information is also available on Workright at *http://www.dti.gov.uk/workright/*, the Working Times Directive, including a frequently asked questions section which gives guidance to both employers and employees.

The site itself, the Department claims, is always being expanded with new information, and you can find a "What's New" with links to the new information made available at *http://www.dti.gov.uk/whatsnew.htm*. Part of the Department's site also contains the Invest in Britain section, which aims to encourage more investment and money to come Britain's way. The site at *http://www.dti.gov.uk/ibb/* details why Britain is the best country to invest in and it is a very creditable and well-designed site.

One of the more useful sites linked to the Trade and Industry site is Companies House at *http://www.companies-house.gov.uk/*, which contains a free searchable database of all limited and public limited companies in the United Kingdom, including their date of formation and details of when accounts are due. Although the search facility is only available during normal working hours, it is a very informative service, and if further information is required about a limited company, the accounts can be ordered for a fee.

The Department of Trade is one of those departments which lists a large number of documents on its web-site which are neither available on-line, nor can be requested by e-mail. Although this problem is gradually solved every day by the emergence of more on-line documents, it cannot be entirely cost effective for a department to print publications for free and pay for postage, when that same document could have been delivered on-line at a minimal charge.

Treasury

Department web site: *http://www.hm-treasury.gov.uk/*
Ministerial: *http://www.hm-treasury.gov.uk/pub/html/profiles/main.html*
Press releases: *http://www.hm-treasury.gov.uk/news.html*
Responsibilities: *http://www.hm-treasury.gov.uk/hmt.html*
Speeches: *http://www.hm-treasury.gov.uk/speech/chex.html*

The Treasury is run by the Chancellor of the Exchequer, currently Gordon Brown. Before the last General Election, the Treasury site and the Foreign Office web-sites were generally acknowledged to be the best Government sites around. It is disappointing that the latest version of the Treasury site seems to have become more drab and it is harder to locate information. Most of the web-pages have very long URLs, but hidden amongst the pages there is a range of valuable information.

It would be nice to see a Treasury site which has a lot of statistical figures available for the economist to come along and get excited about. The latest economic statistics are available linked from the front-page of this site, but they are hardly informative or easy to understand, and there is little information given to the reader to help them compare the statistics either with other countries, or with previous years. It would be nice to see better listings telling us the latest interest rates, inflation rates and so on in easily accessible table format. You can however find the Government's economic strategy, and this is linked from the main index page of the site. There is a long summary of what areas the Treasury is focusing on and the results and costings of the actions which they plan to take.

Love it or loathe it, the Euro is becoming more and more important to British business after its introduction in Europe. The Treasury has set up a web-site which helps businesses and individuals prepare for the Euro in foreign transaction dealings, and explains what the Euro means in practical terms. The site at *http://www.euro.gov.uk/* answers in detail what the Government's policy is on the Euro, and gives general advice on how to find out more information.

Speeches by the Chancellor and his fellow Ministerial team can be found at *http://www.hm-treasury.gov.uk/speech/chex.html.* It is disappointing to see that there are no speeches for the last six months (funnily enough the period from when Charlie Whelan left as press officer for the Chancellor), although a note on the site says that they are being made available soon.

Other sites linked to the Treasury, are the Financial Services Authority (*http://www.fsa.gov.uk/*), the Inland Revenue (*http://www.open. gov.uk/inrev/irhome.htm*) and Customs and Excise (*http://www.hmce. gov.uk/*), which are all featured elsewhere in this directory. The Bank of England site, which is also featured elsewhere in this directory, is a very well-designed site with a range of interesting information at *http://www.bankofengland.co.uk/.*

One of the biggest flaws with this site, although the site claims this is under review, is that there are very few departmental documents available on-line. The titles can be found with some searching, but it would be a valuable additional to open and free Government if more economic papers were added to the site over the coming months.

Department of Social Security

Department web page: *http://www.dss.gov.uk/*
Ministerial info: *http://www.dss.gov.uk/hq/ministers/mainframe.htm*
Press releases: *http://www.dss.gov.uk/hq/press/mainframe.htm*
Responsibilities: *http://www.dss.gov.uk/hq/index.htm*
Speeches: *http://www.dss.gov.uk/hq/press/mainframe.htm*

Although not the best looking of web-sites, the Department of Social Security's site does come with a useful summary to its contents at *http://www.dss.gov.uk/siteguid.htm.* This enables the site to be split into the Benefits Agency, the Contributions Agency, the Child Support Agency, DSS Headquarters and the War Pensions Agency.

The Benefits Agency home-page at *http://www.dss.gov.uk/ba/ index.htm* contains details of the work of the agency, and contains a large number of documents in .pdf format. There are a series of maps to click on to obtain details of where your local office is, as well as the latest press releases for the agency. Although not fully comprehensive by any means, this is a useful web-site which has made available the content most people would expect to see on the pages.

Following a departmental change of responsibilities, most of the information about the Contributions Agency can now be found at *http://www.inlandrevenue.gov.uk/*.

The Child Support Agency home-page at *http://www.dss.gov.uk/csa/ index.htm* has a whole range of publications and contact details, as well as a useful frequently asked questions section. The site has been nicely designed and its compact nature should enable users to find the information they require relatively efficiently.

The DSS Headquarters at *http://www.dss.gov.uk/hq/index.htm* contains all the press releases for the department, Ministerial information, speeches and reports. The biographies of the Ministerial team are very short however, and there are disappointingly few speeches made available. There used to be a very useful facts and figures section a *http://www.dss.gov.uk/hq/index.htm*, but the site reports that the information is now "out-of-date and cannot be relied upon". Hopefully the correct information will be presented on the site soon.

The War Pensions Agency at *http://www.dss.gov.uk/wpa/index.htm* has a very slow site because of the number of graphics, but like other agencies of the department, the information that most users would expect to find has been made available, including contact addresses, publications and policies.

Also from the main page of the site, you can see reports made about the running and management of a number of benefits agencies and related bodies around the country, with the reports being made available in full.

REGIONAL DEPARTMENTS

Scotland

Following devolution the Scottish Office, the Welsh Office and the Northern Ireland Office have all had powers transferred away from them, and the web-sites are starting to reflect that.

In Scotland, if you are unsure of what Governmental authority you need to contact, a web-site at *http://www.scotland.gov.uk/* has been set up to provide information on the new Parliament and its powers. The Scottish Office web-site itself has information on what powers it retains since the shift in responsibilities and which have been given to the new Parliament. There is also limited information on the Ministerial team, speeches and the department's press releases.

There is also a nice section which covers the history of Scotland since 1609 at *http://194.247.69.28/overview/history.htm* which is well-presented and contains interesting information about how power has shifted between London and Scotland over the last few centuries.

Wales

The Welsh Office web-site seems to have disappeared from *http://www.wales.gov.uk/* to be replaced with the National Assembly web-site which seemingly just lists endless self-promoting press releases. However the present site is generally well-presented and does have a range of useful documents about how the Assembly works, and who the members of the assembly are.

Northern Ireland

The Northern Ireland Office web-site at *http://www.nio.gov.uk/* is a very well-presented site which is updated on most days. The Governmental structure in Northern Ireland is quite a complex one, but there is a clear and helpful explanation at *http://www.nio.gov.uk/strucgov.htm*. The present Secretary of State, Mo Mowlam and her Ministers have an information page available at *http://www.nio.gov.uk/mowlam.htm*.

INSTITUTIONAL SITES

Downing St.

In 1996, John Major decided to get in on the act, feeling that if every Government department had a web-site, then why shouldn't he? So a web-site for 10 Downing Street was set up at *http://www.number-10.gov.uk/*. The site was very short on actual information when it opened, although it did contain an interesting guided tour. After the 1997 General Election, there was a long period before the biography of Tony Blair was added to the site, but the site was "upgraded" very badly making it very slow and cumbersome to use. The complaints were listened to, and the page is now faster as well as being increased in both length and scope. Mr Blair learned a harsh lesson about the Internet - that image isn't everything, and content and reliability is more important. Maybe that lesson will spread throughout Government generally!

The disadvantage for the site creators of the Downing Street site was that if they didn't put a contact e-mail address for people to contact the Prime Minister, then there would be much negative press about it being just for show, whereas if they did put an e-mail address, then they would be swamped. In the end, they put a link in to a guest book so that people could leave their comments.

Parliament

The British Parliament's official web-site can be found at *http://www.parliament.uk/*, and this contains links to the House of Lords and House of Commons web-sites. This site has been built for its textual content, not for its graphical quality, but nothing more is required. This site contains some of the most important text that those interested in British politics can find, as a large amount of publications from both the Lords and the Commons can be found, including Hansard.

The House of Commons site at *http://www.parliament.uk/commons/hsecom.htm* has the committee reports as well as Hansard. These publications can be found at *http://www.parliament.the-stationery-office.co.uk/pa/cm/cmpubns.htm*. If you want further information on who your MP is, this is broken down by constituency at *http://www.parliament.uk/commons/lib/alcal.htm*, and general contact details are also given.

Additionally at the House of Commons site, there is a section which lists all the Members of Parliament, the Ministers and also gives details of the Register of Member's Interest, and can be found at *http://www.parliament.uk/commons/cminfo.htm*. From this link, you can also find details of each of the House of Commons committees, and also their membership make-up.

The House of Lords site at *http://www.parliament.the-stationery-*

office.co.uk/pa/ld/ldhome.htm has rather a long-winded URL, but the contents more than make up for this small foible. There is an additional section at *http://www.parliament.the-stationery-office.co.uk/pa/l d199697/ldinfo/ldmeminf.htm*, which lists all the members of the House of Lords, giving not just the name and political party, but also the attendance ratings in both the Chamber itself and also in the committees. Details of new Peerages are also given on this site, as well as general information about the House of Lords itself

Monarchy

The Queen also has a web-site on behalf of the Monarchy at *http://www.royal.gov.uk/*. This web-site is one of the most visited set of pages in the country, which confirms just how many people around the world are interested in our Monarchy. The number of accesses to the Monarchies of other countries is substantially lower. Whether this is because people around the world respect the tradition and position of the Monarchy, or they have essays which they have to write on the subject remains to be seen.

The site itself has excellent content about the Monarchy and its work. There is a very useful historical section at *http://www.royal. gov.uk/history/index.htm*, which has family trees and details of all the Monarchs since 802. The biographies of previous Monarchs are very useful to students, as is a great deal of the information across the site, especially the questions and answers section. The site has won this directory's best politically related site on the Internet, possibly slightly ironic for an institution which has to be politically independent.

Available on the Royal web-site is a permanent section dedicated to Diana, Princess of Wales. These web-pages which can be found at *http://www.royal.gov.uk/start.htm*, have recorded the details of the funeral service as well as a biography of the Princess who died in 1997. You can also see the Queen's message and the words said by other people after the sudden death of Diana.

If you think "Your business is good enough" then visit *http://www. queensawards.org.uk/* where you can find out more information about the Queen's Awards. The number of accesses to this site is very low judging by their own access counter, but the site does provide all the information you need to see to ascertain whether you are suitable to apply, and then details of how to apply.

In early 1999, the Queen was joined on-line by the Prince of Wales, who set up a site at *http://www.princeofwales.gov.uk/*. There are regular on-line forums, which at the moment is on whether we should be using GM foods. There are various news articles and press releases, as well as the engagements of Prince Charles. There is a picture gallery section at *http://www.princeofwales.gov.uk/gallery/latest/*, and the speeches of Prince Charles are available at *http://www.prince ofwales.gov.uk/speeches/*, which unlike many of sites has a useful search feature where you search by key-words or dates.

Both of the previous sites link to Royal Insight at *http://www.royalinsight.gov.uk/*, which is an on-line magazine about the life and work of the British Royal family. This is a superbly presented web-site which allows you to put your questions, find out the engagements of the members of the Royal Family, as well as catch up on the various pieces of news and events. Although unlikely to contain gossip about members of the Royal Family, it is a very valuable life-style type site.

The Commonwealth has an on-line presence at *http://www.tcol.co.uk/* which has introductory details of the work of the Commonwealth and which has not just a comprensive list of all the member countries, but also large amounts of detail about each country's political, geographical and economic situation.

The Official Site of the Historical Royal Palaces at *http://www.hrp .org.uk/* is a professional looking site, but it suffers from being quite slow to load. There is information on a number of Palaces, from the Tower of London to Kensington Palace. Details of each Palace, and what special events and features can be seen in each, can be found. There is a game at *http://www.hrp.org.uk/quiz/newuser.htm* where you have to answer questions about the different Royal Palaces. Although this isn't hugely complex, it is mildly entertaining for a short while.

Church of England
The Archbishop of Canterbury has a site at *http://www.archbishopofcanterbury.org/*, although it doesn't appear to be as well-known as some of the other institutional sites. At the site you can find details of the George Carey as well as list of previous Archbishops at *http://www.archbishopofcanterbury.org/success.htm*.

SOME OF THE OTHER INSTITUTIONS

In addition to these large institutional sites, there are a range of smaller Government departments or official bodies. Here are just a few

Accounts Commission for Scotland
http://www.scot-ac.gov.uk/

Judging by the access counter on this page, it seems to have a low number of visitors, but the site is well-presented although a little slow, and contains information on how the commission works, and how to find out more about the body. The annual report is available, but only in .pdf format.

A.C.A.S
http://www.acas.org.uk/

The ACAS (the Advisory, Conciliation and Arbitration Service) web-site has a range of their publications on-line, as well as contact details to their various offices. They also regularly update what events they have in various parts of the country.

Bank of England
http://www.bankofengland.co.uk/

Parts of this site contain almost excessive amounts of economic terminology and data, but in reality, this means that the site is immensely useful for those who wish to properly research the economy and how the Bank of England fits into that. For those that wish to understand the terminology, the Bank has made efforts to describe each term and try to simplify the process for beginners.

Other sections of the web-site are much more readable, and some are quite interesting, which is impressive for what could have so easily been quite a staid site. On a sub-section of the Bank site at *http://www.bankofengland.co.uk/funny.htm*, there are some humorous stories about the history of the Bank of England.

One of these stories includes details about how, in 1836, the Bank received an anonymous letter from a member of the public who said he could gain access to the bank vaults. They were not convinced at first, but they agreed to meet at a pre-determined time, and they found to their concern that simply by lifting a few floor-boards you could gain access to the bank vaults from the sewers. The sewer-man who found out the information hadn't stolen anything from the vaults, but was generously rewarded for his honesty.

Blood Service
http://www.blooddonor.org.uk/

One politician once said that the worst thing about being an MP was that there is a moral obligation to give blood as it was something that would look bad in their local constituency to decline. For those who wish to give blood without needing such public pressure, this site has a questions and answers section, such as that if you feel faint after giving blood, don't climb up a ladder. You can view the stocks of blood available each week by type at *http://www.bloodnet.nbs.nhs.uk/stats.asp.*

British Council
http://www.britcoun.org/

One of the nicest looking web-sites, this site manages to maintain a professional look without compromising on the speed of the pages. The British Council performs a wide number of roles, including presiding over examinations, running information libraries and supporting arts and educational projects in 109 countries.

British Museum
http://www.british-museum.ac.uk/

At time of writing, large parts of this web-site were still under construction. Currently there are floor plans, details of exhibitions and general information about the running of and access to the Museum. The British Museum has a project called COMPASS (Collections Multimedia Public Access System) which is ready to be launched in the museum itself. Hopefully in years to come, the information from this project might be available on-line.

Building Research Authority
http://www.bre.co.uk/
The BRE was purchased from the Government in 1997, and is now owned by the non-profit making Foundation for the Built Environment. Most of the news-letters are available on-line in .pdf format, and there are contact details should to you wish to find out more about the work of the authority.

Customs and Excise
http://www.hmce.gov.uk/c&ehome.htm

The Custom and Excise's information service pages are very comprehensive, and list in great detail the publications which the department has available. Most of these are available on-line which is a substantial improvement on a number of other web-sites. However, at the time of writing there are a large number of broken links which could be frustrating when looking for information.

Engineering Council
http://www.engc.org.uk/

Despite an ugly background on the front page of this site, the Engineering council has been accepted as the official voice of the industry to the Government. There are some very useful pages which detail the role they play in Governmental policy making and their influence.

English Heritage
http://www.english-heritage.org.uk/

This site is graphically quite intensive, making it rather slow, although there are details of every English Heritage property in the country. There aren't many policy documents available, just a small link to where publications can be purchased. It would be useful to see a heritage section on the site with the opinions of the organisation on a number of matters, such as how to conserve important monuments in the future, and what role they think they themselves will play in the future.

Environment Agency
http://www.environment-agency.gov.uk/

The Environment Agency is one of the largest agencies and took over the power of numerous smaller organisations which had previously existed. There is, in their words, a "Plain English guide to what we do" which is genuinely very useful as it summaries their work and their responsibilities, as well as providing the relevant contact material. Also on this site is the "Hall of Shame" at *http://www.environment-agency.gov.uk /files/shame.htm* where the agency shames those companies which have done damage to the environment, and it lists the fines that they have received. At the moment, ICI heads this hall of shame.

Financial Services Authority
http://www.fsa.gov.uk/

This body was set up by the Government to monitor the financial industry, and has a well-presented site which contains information about how the Authority runs, its tasks and details of how people can recover their money if any financial business fails.

Human Fertilisation Authority
http://www.hfea.gov.uk/

The HFA is a statutory body which regulates and licenses fertility treatments. Although there are a large number of abbreviations used across the site, these are explained in a very helpful glossary at *http://www.hfea.gov.uk/glossary/index.htm.*

Independent Television Commission
http://www.itc.org.uk/

This commission licenses and regulates British commercial television. The site is designed to enable smooth navigation, and there is a substantial amount of information available across this site. The annual performance review is available for nearly every ITV company in Word and Excel format.

National Audit Office
http://www.open.gov.uk/nao/home.htm

This site is very simply designed, but contains details of all the reports which the National Audit Office produces each year. At the moment the site is held back by the fact that none of these publications are available on-line other than in very basic summary, it would add substantially to the site if it became possible to make the full text available on the Internet. The site also contains details of vacancies in the department, and gives information about their graduate recruitment program.

Royal Mint
http://www.royalmint.com/

On 1 April 1997 the Royal Mint became an Executive Agency, which enabled it to maintain its position as official producer of the British coinage, but also giving it more commercial freedom. The site itself might look graphically well-presented, but it is very slow-loading throughout. There are a series of short, but useful, pages about the history and functioning of the Royal Mint which can be accessed from the facts and figures section.

SECTION FIVE

Censorship on the Internet

The Internet worries some politicians. It's not that they don't like the idea of the Internet, they talk a lot about promoting its usage, and of making it available in every school and eventually every home in the land. But when it actually comes round to it, politicians do worry.

They have good reason to, the Internet is a very powerful resource. In December 1997, the identity of the Cabinet Minister's son who had sold cannabis was revealed. Without the Internet, Jack Straw might not have had quite the media attention he did. If that sort of information worries individual politicians, Governments have much more to fear. MI5 whistle-blower, David Shayler, set up his own web-site to tell the world exactly what he thought they should know. The Government wasn't pleased.

The Internet worries the police as well as the security forces. With the invention of secure servers and encrypted mail, it is just about impossible to actually break into an e-mail which is sent encrypted. The French didn't like this, claiming it was a risk to national security, criminals could not be caught was the warning, and the politicians worried again. It took a concerted campaign by a large number of people and some well-organised pressure groups to prevent the British Government taking similar action in 1999.

In early 1999, someone posted details of British members of the security forces stationed abroad. Although the British Government got the site taken down immediately, mirror sites had already been set up, making the task of totally removing this information from the Internet almost impossible.

So politicians have been made to feel vulnerable about the Internet in a number of ways, and their first reaction might be to start censoring the Internet. It seems that the Government can never quite trust us with free speech.

SITES OF INTEREST

Al Gore
http://www.gore2000.gov/

This was the scene of "Goregate", where Al Gore was found to have funded this web-site using White House resources.

Shayler Web-Site
http://www.shayler.com/

This site caused a lot of controversy in late 1998 when David Shayler, a former MI5 employee, decided to become a whistle-blower. He found himself in France and able to write a web-site about his experiences. The Government could stop newspapers publishing his stories, but it couldn't stop people talking about it on the Internet.

Starr Report Analysis
http://www.interngate.com/

This site was one of the sites which received massive audiences in the White House scandal which followed the Starr Report. This site was receiving around one million accesses a day, Internet users don't mind reading about scandal, it's just the politicians that are a little worried about that.

Lobbying Companies

Lobbying companies have had a bad press recently with the media talking about them buying MPs and giving cash payments for asking questions. However, lobbying companies aim to provide advice to business and charities on how to get their point across to our elected representatives, and how to do it in the most efficient manner. Currently, there are no very large web-sites for any lobbying companies but there are some well-designed small ones available.

Should you wish to find out more about the latest set of political lobbyists, Punch Magazine has a long article on-line, available at *http://www.punch.co.uk/millbank.html*. It concentrates on how after years of political lobbyists being linked to the Conservative Party, a new wave has appeared to concentrate on charming New Labour.

Not very many of the lobbying companies have gone on-line, and very few have web-sites which tell us much company. In comparison with the US, where large numbers of lobbying companies have large sites there is a noticeable difference. It might just be the British lagging behind the Americans as we do in other Internet areas, or it might be because of the way that lobbying companies are still treated with some, largely undeserved, disdain by parts of the British media.

APCO
http://www.apco.co.uk/

The APCO site was one of the first lobbying company web-sites that went on-line. It was one of the most graphically appealing, and had a selection of information about Government that was of use. However, the site hasn't been updated significantly in terms of the additional resources available, but it does remain a well-designed and well-presented site for the company, which details its British and European activities.

GJW
http://www.gjw.co.uk/

GJW are one of the largest political lobbying companies in Europe, and they have a very effective site which explains their world-wide operations. There are detailed profiles of the key staff and explanations of what the company can do, and the specialisms which it has.

Here are a few of the other lobbyists and political services:

Beattie Media Public Affairs
http://www.beattiemedia.co.uk

A S Biss & Co
http://www.asbiss.demon.co.uk

AUGUST.ONE Public Affairs
http://www.augustone.com

Bruce Naughton Wade
http://bnw.co.uk

Burson Marsteller Public Affairs
http://www.bm.com

Campaign Information
http://www.politics.co.uk

Citigate Westminster
http://www.citigate.com

DeHaviland Public Affairs
http://www.dehaviland.co.uk

EPPA
http://www.eppa.com

Grant Butler Coomber
http://www.grantbutler.com

Ludgate Public Affairs
http://www.ludgate.co.uk

Politics International
http://www.politicsint.co.uk

Randalls Parliamentary Service
http://www.parliamentary-data-online.co.uk

Think-Tanks

Policy ideas don't just come out of thin air. Associated loosely to each wing of political thought, there are a range of think tanks, which think up some of the more interesting policy proposals. An increasing number of the think-tanks have taken the step of going on-line, and most will gain from this by being able to sell their publications. A few of the organisations have started to make some of their publications available on-line, and this is especially valuable for students of politics.

Adam Smith Institute
http://www.adamsmith.org.uk/

This web-site is initially split up into the policy and international divisions. The policy division has a very bright background which surprisingly works quite well. There is a substantial amount of information available at this web-site, including your chance to buy an Adam Smith mouse-mat or baseball cap (you too can look like William Hague) at *http://www.adamsmith.org.uk/policy/toys.htm*. There are details as to how you can purchase the Institute's publications, and the Institute's bulletins are also available on-line.

The international division of this has details of what the Institute can do in countries abroad. It details the training and advisory services which it can provide, whilst still following the principles of the Adam Smith Institute in Britain.

Centre For European Reform
http://www.cer.org.uk/

Centre for Policy Studies
http://www.cps.org.uk/

This right-wing think-tank was founded in 1974 by Margaret Thatcher and the late Keith Joseph. It takes credit for a number of policies such as privatisation, education reform and the sale of council houses. The web-site has a number of speeches available to download, and contains brief summaries from articles in its latest magazines which can be purchased. There is also a calendar of events and links to other sites of interest.

Centre for Reform
http://www.cfr.org.uk/

The Centre for Reform is a new public policy think tank pursuing the values of the Liberal Democrats. The web-site is well-presented, but there are small sections of the site which are out-of-date and the odd link doesn't function correctly. The site contains useful details on the publications and events of the institution. The navigation of the site easy and there is a comprehensive list of links provided to other sites of interest, and because of this, the Centre For Reform has won a place in this directory's top ten web-sites.

Demos
http://www.demos.co.uk/

The Economist called Demos "the most influential think tank in Britain" and their site presents details of their latest events and provides information about their publications. Demos have split their publications into easy to navigate sections by topic which makes finding the right document much easier.

Fabian Society
http://www.fabian-society.org.uk/

The Fabian Society have a very large web-site with in-depth pages about their aims and events. The Fabian Society's publications are probably better known than those from many other think-tanks, but although there is a list on-line of the publications which have been produced, it is sometimes slow and cumbersome to actually find the publications that you are interested in. You can also join the Society's mailing list free of charge from the site.

Hansard Society
http://www.hansard-society.org.uk/

This web-site by the prestigious Hansard Society concentrates mainly on training courses which it makes available to foreign students. Although the Society publishes a number of documents, very little detail of these are given, although details are given on how you can order the hard copies.

Institute for Public Policy Research
http://www.ippr.org.uk/

The Institute for Public Policy Research is a centre-left organisation. Their web-site, which could possibly be improved in terms of presentation, provides the standard contact details, but doesn't provide much information on their publications, although the hard copies can be purchased through the web-site.

Institute of Economic Affairs
http://www.iea.org.uk/

The Institute, founded in 1955, aims to promote the "educating of the British public in the knowledge of economic and social problems and their solutions". The site is very well-presented, and there is a comprehensive section on the history of the institute, something missing from a number of the other sites. There are a few pages which currently are empty, but otherwise this is one of the best sites of its type.

John Stuart Mill Institute
http://websites.ntl.com/~julian.wates/JSMI_Site/

This think tank is a independent organisation based on the traditional liberal values. The web-site is kept up-to-date, with details of events and publications of the Institute, including the annual John Stuart Mill Lecture.

Nexus
http://www.netnexus.org/

Initially this site looks short on content from the index pages, and the design looks very plain. However, a short exploration into the site to http://www.netnexus.org/library/author.htm and you to see a considerable list of documents which have been produced by Nexus. Unlike a number of other groups, a considerable amount of actual text is available without ordering having to order hard copies of documents.

Royal Institute of International Affairs
http://www.riia.org/

This institute aims to promote the understanding of international affairs. To their credit, they have made the contents of their research papers available on-line, and have provided details of how to order the more substantial documents they produce. The design of the pages is very simple, mainly relying on text links, but it is easy to navigate around this site and find the information that you require.

Social Market Foundation
http://www.smf.co.uk/

This is a well-presented site which provides a range of information about the Foundation, as well as having their news-letter and certain leaflets available on-line. There are also comprehensive contact details, and general information about the aims of the Foundation.

UK Citizen's On-line Democracy
http://www.democracy.org.uk/

This site received a lot of publicity after the 1997 General Election. It aims to be the first on-line pressure group and think-tank, and it includes a foreword from the Prime Minister, Tony Blair.

E-Mail a Politician

From experience, I know that these e-mail addresses change frequently, and are sometimes unavailable. If an e-mail address doesn't work, it might be worth re-sending it once to see if it gets through a second time.

As I mentioned in the introduction to the directory, there are ways to e-mail your MP (or to at least try to) if their name doesn't appear below, but don't be too hopeful. If you do know of any more MPs who have e-mail other than those below, please let me know. I will have to check firstly though that the MP in question is willing to have his or her e-mail published.

The other alternative method to find out an MP's e-mail address, and this is usually only the last resort, is to write to them at the House of Commons, Westminster, London, SW1 and ask them if they have an e-mail address which you can use. If they have, then you have your answer, and if not, your very asking has made the MP realise that there is at least some demand for them to acquire an e-mail address for constituency correspondence.

A further note about contacting MPs. If you require help, then the House of Commons procedure dictates that you should in the first instance contact your constituency MP so that they can help you with your problem, or forward the query on if necessary. So do not contact, at least in the first instance, another MP as they will be very restricted in how they can help you.

The e-mail addresses supplied below are for contacting your constituency MP, or an MP who you wish to contact directly. They are not for sending large mass mailings to. From your point of view, these are ineffective and largely a waste of time, the person reading the e-mail will realise it is a circular and deal with it in the same way as they deal with most of the other circulars the MP receives. From the point of view of democracy generally, it doesn't encourage politicians to get an e-mail address, or publicise it if they are continually abused with large amounts of junk mail.

THE LIST OF E-MAIL ADDRESSES

Conservative Party

Arbuthnot, James	arbuthnotj@parliament.uk
Baldry, Tony	baldrt@parliament.uk
Bercow, John	bercowj@parliament.uk
Chapman, Sir Sydney	BarnetCon@aol.com
Day, Stephen	stephen.day@zetnet.co.uk
Evans, Nigel	ribblevalley@dial.pipex.com
Taylor, Ian	taylor@mintech.demon.co.uk
Whittingdale, John	jwhittingdale.mp@email.tory.org.uk
Young, Sir George	sir-george-young@nwh-tories.org.uk

Labour Party

Ainsworth, Robert	ainsworthr@parliament.uk
Allen, Graham	graham.allen@geo2.poptel.org.uk
	alleng@parliament.uk
Anderson, Janet	janet.anderson@culture.gov.uk
Armstrong, Hilary	armstrong@parliament.uk
Atherton, Candy	atherton@parliament.uk
Atkins, Charlotte	atkinsc@parliament.uk
Banks, Tony	tony.banks@culture.gov.uk
Battle, John	john_battle_mp@lab-sci.demon.co.uk
Bayley, Hugh	bayleyh@parliament.uk
Bell, Stuart	bells@parliament.uk
Benn, Tony	bennt@parliament.uk
Bennett, Andrew	andrew.bennett@geo2.geonet.de
Berry, Roger	berryr@parliament.uk
Blair, Tony	tony.blair@geo2.poptel.org.uk
Campbell, Anne	Anne.Campbell.MP@dial.pipex.com

Cunningham, Jack	jack.cunningham@geo2.poptel.org.uk
Dobson, Frank	frank.dobson@geo2.poptel.org.uk
Dunwoody, Gwynnneth	dunwoodyg@aol.com
Eagle, Angela	angela.eagle.mp@mcr1.geonet.de
Grant, Bernie	Bernie.Grant@poptel.org.uk
Griffiths, Nigel	104074.3105@compuserve.com
Hall, Michael	michael.hall@geo2.poptel.org.uk
Hogg, Norman	100305.607@compuserve.com
Hoon, Geoff	geoffrey.hoon@geo2.poptel.org.uk
Howarth, Alan	alan.howarth@culture.gov.uk
Jones, Fiona	jones@newlab.u-net.com
Keen, Alan	alank@patrol.i-way.co.uk
Keen, Ann	akeen@patrol.i-way.co.uk
Livingstone, Ken	105277.3653@compuserve.com
Meale, Alan	alan.meale@geo2.poptel.org.uk
Miller, Andrew	andrew.miller@geo2.poptel.org.uk
Moran, Margaret	moranm@parliament.uk
Raysnford, Nick	seabeckaj@parliament.uk
Rooker, Jeff	jeff.rooker@geo2.poptel.org.uk
Short, Clare	shortc@parliament.uk
Smith, Chris	chris.smith@culture.gov.uk
Timms, Stephen	100746.2456@compuserve.com
Wyatt, Derek	wyattd@parliament.uk

Liberal Democrats

Allan, Richard	ric_allan@cix.co.uk
Ashdown, Paddy	paddyashdown@cix.compulink.co.uk
Baker, Norman	normanbaker@cix.co.uk
Ballard, Jackie	jackieballard@cix.co.uk
Beith, Alan	berwicklibdems@cix.co.uk
Brake, Tom	cwlibs@cix.co.uk
Brand, Peter	alexfolkes@cix.co.uk
Breed, Colin	wilsone@cix.co.uk
Bruce, Malcolm	gordonlibdems@cix.compulink.co.uk
Burnett, John	torrwdevonld@cix.co.uk
Burstow, Paul	pburstow@cix.co.uk
Cable, Vincent	lnmann@cix.co.uk
Campbell, Menzies	nefifelibdem@cix.compulink.co.uk
Chidgey, David	eastleighldp@cix.compulink.co.uk

Cotter, Brian	westonlibdems@cix.co.uk
Davey, Edward	eddavey@cix.co.uk
Davies, Chris	olde_sadd_ldp@cix.compulink.co.uk
Fearn, Ronnie	southportldp@cix.co.uk
Foster, Don	donfostermp@cix.compulink.co.uk
George, Andrew	stivesldp@cix.co.uk
Gorrie, Donald	edinwestldp@cix.co.uk
Hancock, Mike	portsmouthldp@cix.co.uk
Harris, Evan	neilfawcett@cix.co.uk
Harvey, Nick	nickharveymp@cix.compulink.co.uk
Heath, David	davidheath@cix.co.uk
Hughes, Simon	bermondsey@cix.co.uk
Jones, Nigel	nigeljonesmp@cix.compulink.co.uk
Keeth, Paul	herlibdem@cix.co.uk
Kirkwood, Archie	archiekirkwood@cix.compulink.co.uk
MacLennan, Bob	bobmaclennan@cix.compulink.co.uk
Moore, Michael	michaelmoore@cix.co.uk
Oaten, Mark	moaten@cix.co.uk
Opik, Lembit	fionahall@cix.co.uk
Rendel, David	newburyldp@cix.compulink.co.uk
Russell, Bob	tsutton@cix.co.uk
Sanders, Adrian	torbaympoffice@cix.co.uk
Smith, Bob	bobsmith@cix.co.uk
Stunell, Andrew	andrewstunell@cix.co.uk
Tonge, Jenny	jtonge@cix.co.uk
Tyler, Paul	paultylermp@cix.compulink.co.uk
Webb, Steve	stevewebb@cix.co.uk
Wallace, Jim	jimwallace@cix.compulink.co.uk
Willis, Phil	johnfox@cix.co.uk

Scottish National Party

Cunningham, Roseanna	rcmp.perth@snp.org.uk
Salmond, Alex	asmp.peterhead@snp.org.uk
Welsh, Andrew	awmp.arbroath@snp.org.uk

Independent

Bell, Martin	bellm@parliament.uk

Members of the European Parliament

Adam, Gordon	100305.2120@compuserve.com
Bowe, David	david.bowe@geo2.poptel.org.uk
Crampton, Peter	101457.33%2076@compuserve.com
Cunningham, Tony	tony.cunningham@geo2.poptel.org.uk
Donnelly, Alan	Alan.Donnelly@ping.be
Falconer, Alex	104706.1600@compuserve.com
Ford, Glyn	glynford.euromp@zen.co.uk
Green, Pauline	101361.2350@compuserve.com
Hallam, David	david.hallam@geo2.poptel.org.uk
Hardstaff, Veronica	hardstaff.mepbx@geo2.poptel.org.uk
Harrison, Lyndon	lyndon.harrison@geo2.poptel.org.uk
Hendrick, Mark	m.hendrick.mep@geo2.poptel.org.uk
Hindley, Michael	michael.hindley@mcrl.poptel.org.uk
Howitt, Richard	richard.howitt@geo2.poptel.org.uk
Kerr, Hugh	hugh.kerr@geo2.poptel.org.uk
Kinnock, Glenys	glenys.kinnock@geo2.poptel.org.uk
Martin, David	David_Martin@ccis.org.uk
McCarthy, Arlene	arlene.mccarthy@geo2.poptel.org.uk
McNally, Eryl	eryl.mcnally@geo2.poptel.org.uk
Miller, Bill	bill.miller@geo2.poptel.org.uk
Morgan, Eluned	e.morgan.mep@geo2.poptel.org.uk
Murphy, Simon	simon.murphy@geo2.poptel.org.uk
Newens, Stan	office@newens.demon.co.uk
Pollack, Stan	anita.pollack@geo2.poptel.org.uk
Read, Mel	mel.read@geo2.poptel.org.uk
Smith, Alex	asmithmep@enterprise.net
Tappin, Mike	m.tappin.mep@geo2.poptel.org.uk
Titley, Mike	gary.titley@mcrl.poptel.org.uk
Tomlinson, John	john.tomlinson@geo2.poptel.org.uk
Tongue, Carole	carole.tongue@geo2.poptel.org.uk
Waddington, Sue	101450.2601@compuserve.com
Wilson, Joe	joe.wilson@geo2.poptel.org.uk
Wynn, Terry	terry-wynnmep@geo2.poptel.org.uk

European Internet Sites

Depending on your luck, you should find that you have at least one MEP with an e-mail address (see previous chapter) whom you can e-mail about European issues. You can get an introduction to European issues by looking through the sites in this section, but be warned, it's a very wide area covered by a very many institutions.

Whether or not Britain should play a greater part in Europe, there are a large number of web-sites for those European institutions which have such a major effect on British political life. The creators of these web-sites have a major problem in that they have to make all of the text available in a number of different languages. Additionally, the structures of the European Union and the other bodies are complex, and a number of these sites have made great efforts to explain how each institution fits in with the others.

Firstly, the large site is the European Union's site at *http://www.europa.eu.int/*. The site links to all of the other main European institutions so that the user can understand what's going on. There are press information pages and a large number of the official European Union publications are available on-line. There are instructions for finding those documents which aren't currently on-line, and if you want to know exactly how the European civil service is run (who doesn't?) then there is a wide range of information on this. You can also find the latest details of the Euro, and other economic statistics about the Union and its members.

The European Parliament has its own web-site at *http://www.europarl.eu.int/*, which provides a wide range of Parliamentary news and information, as well as how to get employment and attend European meetings. As yet, the actual debates of the European Parliament aren't available on-line, but this is intended to be added in the future. Lists of all of the European Members of Parliament across Europe are available, and it is interesting to compare how many of our foreign colleagues are on-line, the British contingent compares more than favourably. You can search for members by constituency, country, name, party or committee. The site is actually quite comprehensive in terms of the amount of information available, but it is very difficult to actually find the information that you need. Certain parts of the site also look slightly out-of-date.

One of the sites most eagerly awaited was the Council of Ministers site, which came on-line in 1997. The English version of the site is available at *http://ue.eu.int/en/summ.htm*, and contains information about the body, what it does, and how effectively it works. This site is immensely impressive, with nearly every useful document available on-line. A range of other institutional information is available which links this site into the other European institutional web-sites. Although there are contact details for the staff, e-mail addresses would be beneficial as a point of contact.

The Committee of the Regions' web-site at *http://www.cor.eu.int/* has a meet the members section, and information on the role of the organisation, especially useful as few people realise that the Committee has 222 members. It is slightly disappointing that there are numerous spelling mistakes in the English section. In the future it would be nice to see more of the Committee's publications on-line. At the moment there are only three available for the last three years.

The Council of European Municipalities and Regions at *http://www.ccre.org/* is available only in English and French. There are a number of contact e-mail addresses and details of recent activities of the Council, but it is not always clear exactly what the Council does.

The European Court of Auditors at *http://www.eca.eu.int/*. This site, rather shoddily designed in FrontPage, is short on documents that the institution produces, and is too reliant on documents in .pdf format that it does produce. For an institution committed to open and fair Government in the European Union, there is still substantial work to do on this site.

The statistical office for the European communities is EUROSTAT, and the site is available at *http://europa.eu.int/en/comm/eurostat/euro-stat.html*. The information available in only three languages (English,

French and German) is nowhere near sufficient for most people's purposes. There are many links to places where you can obtain further information, but there is precious little statistical information freely available on-line. There is a .pdf version of the summary produced by EUROSTAT three times a year, but many researchers who visit this site will require more information than is contained in these summaries.

If you ever have a problem with any of the European institutions, you can contact the European Ombudsman at *http://www.euro-ombudsman.eu.int/*. You are given a facility to send your concerns or comments to the Ombudsman by e-mail, and there are numerous helpful factsheets which detail how you can complain and get your problems independently assessed.

If you want news regarding the information revolution being brought about in Europe, you can visit *http://www.ispo.cec.be/*. This is the site of ISPO, which aims to promote the efforts of the European Union with regard to tele-working, e-commerce and on-line commercial developments.

Finally, the European Convention for Protection of Pet Animals, a small but admirable organisation, has a web-site at *http://www.cdb.org.uk/euro.htm*.

Internet News-groups

USENET news-groups are just perfect for those interested in politics on the Internet. You can join in a huge number of political debates covering nearly every country in the world, and hundreds of different topics. You can be as anonymous as you want, or as open as you want. For those with a love of arguments and debates, you could well find (assuming you can cope with the typing and abuse) yourself literally tearing yourself away from the computer at times. USENET is addictive.

For those discussing British politics, you first port of call is the uk.politics groups. The fore-runner of these groups was *uk.politics* itself, a newsgroup finally disappeared in 1995 to be replaced by lots of smaller groups, such as *uk.politics.misc*, *uk.politics.constitution*, *uk.politics.drugs*, *uk.politics.parliament*, *uk.politics.guns*, *uk.politics.animals*, *uk.politics.crime*, *uk.politics.economics* and so the list goes on. There is also the newsgroup *alt.politics.british* which is available for those who don't have access to the uk. hierarchies.

The debates can get very abusive, and the level of knowledge that the contributors have varies enormously. Some of the posters believe it is their right to comment on every subject under the sun, with varying degrees of knowledge about it. However, you will find that there are a large number of experts on any particular subject, and it can be a very useful learning resource as well as discussion forum.

If you phrase your query concisely you will find that many posters will go out of their way to help you with any political questions which you might have. In effect you have the ability to ask a question and have it seen by some people who are experts in their field (although be careful for the answers given from those who only feel they are experts), which makes news-groups one of the most versatile academic reference points on the Internet.

If you feel that your area of political interest isn't covered, then you are even able to set up your own newsgroup within the hierarchy. However there are certain procedures which have to be followed and it can be a long process. If you want to create a newsgroup and you feel you are competent with the procedure, visit *uk.net.news-config*. If you feel that there is a political argument to be had and no group to do it in, then there is no reason why you shouldn't go through this process, something I did to create the group *uk.politics.parliament.*

Before shooting off to the news-groups however, take care of all statements which you make on these forums. It is very easy to resort to personal abuse of other posters, and the legal position is still a little unclear. You may run the risk of an expensive legal battle for the comments you had thought were incredibly witty and clever when you posted them.

Even ISPs have been caught up in the problem. A poster to one of the news-groups, Laurence Godfrey, received a lot of publicity after he took legal action against Demon Internet due to comments made by some of their posters. Demon Internet had claimed that they were just innocent passers-on of the information posted by their users, which was rejected by the courts. Try and stay polite and reasonable when you post, which will not only make it far less likely you will have legal action suddenly taken against you, but it will also enhance your reputation on the news-groups anyway.

SITES OF INTEREST

uk.politics. Information Page
http://www.ukpol.co.uk/ukpo.htm

This page gives biographies of some of the leading contributors to the *uk.politics.* groups, and gives information on what groups are available, questions and answers with some of the contributors, and much more. Every month there is also a short biography and question and answer session with a prominent members of one of the *uk.politics.* news-groups.

AOL
http://www.aol.co.uk/

AOL are the largest, at the time of writing, ISP in the world, although they have dropped to being the third largest in the UK after the sudden launch of the free subscription Internet providers. AOL deserve special mention because they have two distinct areas for to those interested in politics, one is the very comprehensive news service which they have on offer which covers not just Britain, but has news-wires available from just about every country in the world.

The other benefit of AOL is that they have numerous chat-rooms you can attend to chat about politics, and you can chat in US rooms about American politics and news, or in UK rooms about British politics and news. The rooms are generally well-attended, and there are set chats at certain times of the week where you can put your point. In addition, in the news section, there are a range of USENET type message boards, such as *ukhomenews* and *worldnews*, where you can leave message about hundreds of different news items for other people to comment on and discuss. As usual with most ISPs, AOL provide a full news feed of all the *uk.politics.** news-groups.

Other Political Sites

Inevitably, there are a selection of sites which don't fit into a distinguishable category, but which all deserve a mention. These range from individuals pursuing their own political belief to institutions which have a relevance to British political life.

The one thing that is important throughout when looking at the sites created by individuals in particular is that it is these are the people who really built the Internet. Without their time and effort, none of the Government institutions would have gone on-line, and none of the progress that has been made would have come about. Some of the sites created by individuals has been mentioned elsewhere in this directory, but it is worth remembering here how important their effort was.

The sites which fit into the vague category of 'other political sites' are arranged into the following six categories: Individuals' Sites, Institutional Sites, Media Sites, Miscellaneous Politics , Police Authorities and Trade Unions.

INDIVIDUAL'S SITES

The Right-to-Work by Sir Ralph Howell
http://www.unemployment.co.uk/

Sir Ralph Howell was the Conservative Member of Parliament for North Norfolk, before he retired at the 1997 General Election. Throughout his time in Parliament, he fought hard for his scheme which offered every individual the right to some form of employment at a reasonable wage level. Although his ideas were never accepted by the last Conservative

Government, the scheme did win much independent praise, and the basic idea of his scheme has been built upon by the present Labour Government with the New Deal scheme.

I asked Sir Ralph about why he set up his web-site, "I feel that society is not doing anything to tackle the root causes of the problem which we face. In countries such as New Zealand, much progress has been made where everyone has a right to work". Sir Ralph also feels that the Internet is a crucial way forward, and despite his age, he is a major supporter of the medium, "I envisage the Internet being much more important in five years time", and "more and more politicians will be forced to use it as an essential means of communication".

The Official Neil Hamilton Web-Site
http://www.neilhamilton.co.uk/

Neil Hamilton is a household name from the allegations of sleaze which were made against him before the 1997 General Election. The Guardian newspaper made a series of allegations against him after Mohammed Fayed made allegations against a number of MPs of taking cash for questions. The main legal battle will be fought at the end of 1999, and this web-site is likely to relay the results of that battle as time progresses.

The site contains many documents, some which are by necessity very complex. Neil Hamilton claims that these show that he isn't guilty of the charges that have been made against him. These are indexed by date for easy accessibility, and not only are there biographies of both Neil and Christine Hamilton, but you can also buy the books written by the couple on-line.

Trial By Conspiracy Web-Site
http://www.coverup.net/

This site was set up Jonathan Boyd Hunt to publicise his book. Hunt believes that Neil Hamilton was unfairly treated by the press, and that the Guardian and Fayed were lying when making their allegations against him. The web-site has some very in-depth documents which require careful reading, but Hunt feels that careful consideration of these documents shows that Neil Hamilton has been unfairly treated.

EUROFAQ - A Euro-Sceptic Resource
http://members.aol.com/eurofaq/

EuroFAQ is written and maintained by an independent group of journalists, businessmen and academics who believe that Britain's membership of the European Union has been a political and economic disaster. The site admits to being one-sided, but unlike many similar sites, this site has proper reference backing for its statements and has a large number of resources and links to further information.

Phil Hunt's Basic Income Site
http://www.vision25.demon.co.uk/pol/bi.htm

The aim of this short but interesting web-page is to "demonstrate that it would be possible to replace the present Social Security system in Britain with a basic income". You can find out more political links from the same author's site at *http://www.vision25.demon.co.uk/pol/zakalwe.htm.*

Sarah Nelson's Leisure Party
http://www.leisureparty.org/sarah.peter.nelson/

This web-site doesn't pretend to be a political party, but is founded on the principle that there is more to life than employment. Sarah Nelson, who created this site with her husband, claims that "I felt compelled to express myself and say, hey, I enjoy being unemployed". It does make a change to see a "party" site which doesn't ask for membership fees to join.

Taking Liberties
http://www.tim1.demon.co.uk/

This web-site, which is run by Tim Walker, and aims to provide information and links to all matters related to civil liberties. There are a series of articles on various civil liberty matters, covering topics as diverse as the British political system to the implications of accepting cookies from web-sites on the Internet.

Tony Blair Dossier
http://www.geocities.com/~journo/blair.html

This web-site, created by Danny Rosenbaum, has a very large collection of documents which are relevant to Tony Blair. Included on this substantial sites are quotes that Blair has made, general Blair information and it also provides such information as who Blair's young advisers are.

INSTITUTIONAL SITES

Adopt an MP
http://www.stand.org.uk/

This is one of the best political web-sites around, it tells the user what it wants to achieve and gives them a positive and innovative way of doing it. It gets into this directory's top ten political web-sites. The group aim to "educate" MPs in this country about sensible methods of encryption, and it has a range of links which provide further information about the subject.

By typing in your post-code, you will be told who your MP is with the option of e-mailing them and also finding out their interests from the Directory of Member's Interests. After this, you will be presented with your own "certificate" with your MP's picture and your e-mail address, which you can then place on your web-site.

Alliance for Worker's Liberty
http://www.workersliberty.org/

This site has a very long front-page, but is filled with information about this group, and has a range of political articles and details political events relevant to their cause. There are also sections of the Worker's Liberty magazine to read on-line.

Campaign Against Censorship of the Internet in Britain
http://www.liberty.org.uk/cacib/

This is a comprehensive site about the political and legal implications of censorship across various sections of the Internet.

Campaign for Press and Broadcasting Freedom
http://www.cpbf.demon.co.uk/

The Campaign for Press and Broadcasting Freedom (CPBF) aims to be an independent voice for media reform, and to make the media more accountable and representative. The site also contains their comprehensive manifesto and details of how to join the organisation, which also aims to allow journalists to be able to report more freely.

Republic
http://www.republic.org.uk/

Republic are an independent pressure group which campaigns to end all forms of hereditary office. Their web-site is very impressive, with a well-designed main page which is fast-loading, and the navigation system which they use is well put together and easy to use. Some pages are slightly out-of-date, but there are useful free news-letters on the site in .pdf format.

United Kingdom Atomic Energy Authority
http://www.ukaea.org.uk/

This well-designed site is run by the UKAEA which was incorporated as a statutory corporation in 1954, and now regulates sections of the nuclear power industry. There are large amounts of information throughout the site, from press releases to useful industrial documents.

THE MEDIA

The media are an important part of the on-line community due to the large sites run by the newspapers and also with the number of researchers and journalists who use the Internet as a key part of their job. The large broad-sheets such as the Telegraph and the Times came onto the Internet very early on, and have made a substantial impact on how people read their news.

The advantage of having a web-site, as well as a printed newspaper, is that the editor can put much more information on the web-site version of the publication. They can put links to sites of interests, long sections from speeches, or unabridged text from manifestos for example. The Times and the Sunday Times manage to do this in the most consistently useful manner. In the years to come, we are likely to see more and more people using the newspaper's web-site as an additional part of the newspaper, not just an on-line copy of it.

Of the newspapers, the following are those which provide a lot of information, which is very up-to-date. Added to that, with most papers you get a comprehensive set of back issues, which can often be searched, and for the moment at least, this is all free of charge. Don't worry if you're asked to register to get access initially, just about all of the main newspaper sites are free to register, although some people have refused to on the grounds of they don't like being watched.

Daily Mirror
http://www.mirror.co.uk/

Possibly not the most glamorous of newspapers, this was one of the first tabloids to go on-line. Indeed, despite the possibilities open to tabloid newspapers on the Internet, the progress they made on actually going on-line was very slow, it was the broad-sheets who had to do all of the running. On this site you can also find the Sunday Mirror and sections of the Sunday People.

A very useful feature to web-designers around the world is the Mirror Picture web-pages at *http://www.mirrorpix.com/*. This enables you to search tens of thousands of images by name or subject, and see photographs of your chosen subject. For a small fee you can buy once-only reproduction rights to that photo by a simple credit-card facility. An immensely useful service which can work out to be very good value.

The Guardian
http://www.guardian.co.uk/

The Guardian was one of the first publications to go on-line. Initially they put their IT section up, and enabled people to e-mail the editors. The site didn't expand much until the following year, when it expanded a lot, and started to encompass the entire newspaper.

On some occasions, the Guardian has put special small web-sites up about certain topics, such as when the Scott report was announced in late 1996. You can also view the Observer from this web-site.

The Independent
http://www.independent.co.uk/

This site contains the on-line version of both The Independent and The Independent on Sunday. Although the entire contents of the paper aren't made available on-line, the users don't have to complete a registration process before being allowed to look around the site.

London Evening Standard
http://www.standard.co.uk/

The latest news and city information is available from the Evening Standard, one of London's largest newspapers. There are also a large number of links with other sites about London, from entertainment to society. The web-site has a large emphasis on London, but the site also has a breaking news section which covers topics from around the world.

The Times & Sunday Times
http://www.sunday-times.co.uk/

This site was first started at the beginning of 1996, and quickly became one of the most popular additions to the Internet. It was one of the first web-sites which brought serious amounts of news to the web. The paper is also noted for putting on nearly its entire contents from the start. Although papers such as the Guardian may have been gone on-line first, they only made a small amount of their news-paper available on-line. You can view a comprehensive archive of past papers from here, as well as access the new Times Money site at *http://www.times-money.co.uk/*.

Daily Telegraph
http://www.telegraph.co.uk/

Along with the Times, this was another one of the first papers to put a large amount of their printed content on-line each and every day. There are a range of different features which are available from the site, in addition to the content which is added at 2am each morning. This site also contains the text of the Sunday Telegraph.

New Scientist
http://www.newscientist.com/

Although this professionally designed site it is mainly a scientific one, they have numerous articles on-line with a political interest, and have an option to perform a comprehensive search on previous issues of the journal.

New Statesman
http://www.newstatesman.co.uk/

This web-site has been recently updated, and tends to follow the general principles of New Labour. There are articles on-line as diverse as classical music and political book reviews, although the site is slightly difficult to navigate.

Tribune
http://www.abel.net.uk/~rost2000/tribune/

Tribune, edited by Mark Seddon, has had an Internet presence for many years, and this site contains details of their current issue, and a list of links to other web-sites of interest. Although it lists Tribune publications, it would be helpful for the readers of the site to have short reviews and details of each one.

Doing It Yourself
As well as existing papers, the Internet is a very good source for new on-line journals to be started. With no start-up costs, anyone can start their own political magazines, and a lot have (although many have found the updating of the site too much and have given up after one issue). One such early on-line magazine was called Insomnia, although this site eventually disappeared, it was a valuable early contribution to "intellectual" on-line political magazines.

MISCELLANEOUS

Abelard On-Line
http://www.abelard.org/

This site, set up by one of the more well-known members, even though he remains anonymous, of the uk.politics hierarchy, aims to put forward educational articles. There are a range of useful resources on this site, and even an explanation of the rather unusual style of writing which the author chooses to use.

Institute of Fiscal Studies
http://www.ifs.org.uk/

The Institute of Fiscal Studies (IFS) is a research institute which is thirty years old in 1999. Its aim is to provide independent economic analysis and research free from political intervention and bias, with special emphasis and research given to the UK's tax system. The site contains detail of how to join, and reproduces the full text of many of its research papers and publications on-line, either in full or in summarised format. The web-site is professionally designed, but could benefit with a glossary to those less familiar with certain economic words and phrases.

Thinking Politica
http://home.freeuk.net/ethos/

This web-site was set up to provide users with a "variety of insights into the social sciences, from political theory to sociology to philosophy".

POLICE AUTHORITIES

Police Services in the UK
http://www.police.uk/

This official site lists all the police authorities in the country, and provides links to all of those with Internet sites. You navigate around the site by clicking on a map of the area you are interested in finding out about, and the maps get progressively more detailed. If the police authority for the area you select has a web-site, then you are automatically taken to it.

Avon & Somerset Constabulary
http://www.avsom.police.uk/

This was one of the first police authorities to develop an on-line presence, and the site works well albeit slightly slowly, providing information on home security, information about the force, as well as details of how to report crimes. Certain sections of the site weren't available when I visited, but the site promised that they would be updated shortly.

Metropolitan Police
http://www.met.police.uk/

This is one of the largest police sites and it has informational content such as contact details and information about the police force works. It also has details of people wanted for various crimes, as well as various press releases which have been issued by the force.

Suffolk Police
http://www.suffolk.police.uk/

Clearly a lot of work has gone into the building of this very impressive looking web-site, but it is disappointing to see from their own figures, that they get only a handful of accesses. Details of the policing plan and various other constabulary services are listed. There is a very nice section of the site at *http://www.suffolk.police.uk/ suffolkpolice/young_people/murder_mystery/index.htm* for youngsters which lets them "take part" in an investigation with pieces of evidence displayed.

TRADE UNIONS

Trade Unions have been generally very slow to enter the on-line medium, and at time of writing, there were a limited number of Trade Unions with web-sites, However there appear to be many more coming.

Amalgamated Engineering and Electrical Union
http://www.aeeu.org.uk/

With 700,000 members, this is one of the largest trade unions in the country. This site is a nice compact site with details of press releases and details of how to join the union. They also have special pages about certain political or electoral events.

Association of University Teachers
http://www.aut.org.uk/

This web-site is tidily produced and contains details of the aims and policies of the union. There are also a number of guidance documents on-line which will be of use to the members of the union.

Currently on the site they have the facility to e-mail various individuals, which they term "the employers" about their pay campaign. Hopefully this kind of activity won't spread to widely, otherwise it will be difficult to persuade more and more politicians to take e-mail communications seriously.

Graphic, Paper and Media Union
http://www.gpmu.org.uk/

This was one of the first trade union sites to go on-line, and they have had a number of interesting campaigns which they have shared on-line. A current one is a "guide to not let the multi-nationals" take over the Internet, but how to "get involved in global cyber-campaigns." The union also makes members aware of any funds available for re-training which might be useful for them.

Knitwear and Footwear Union
http://www.poptel.org.uk/kfat

This union only has 35,000 members, but they have established a small, but reliable web-site. The site is kept up-to-date by the press department, and although it is not going to win awards for graphical presentation, it provides the necessary information for people to join or for those who might need the union's help.

Musician's Union
http://www.musiciansunion.org.uk/

This is a nice bright site with information on joining the union and a very comprehensive section covering frequently asked questions, such as the rights of musicians if their gig is cancelled, and what to do if your neighbours complain that you make too much noise whilst practising.

Scottish Crofter's Union
http://www.scu.co.uk/

With only 4,000 members, this is a relatively tiny Trade Union, but they have compiled an interesting web-site with a history of crofting as well as more traditional information such as joining and contact details. There is a useful section to see the political aims of the union, as well as the progress which they have been able to make so far.

TGWU
http://www.tgwu.org.uk/

This is the best presented trade union site about. It is currently largely under construction, and hopefully they will try and work on making the pages faster to load. The web-site is built around a newspaper type feel, with articles and information on a front-page with a number of photographs which you can click on for further information.

TUC
http://www.tuc.org.uk/

The Trade Unions Congress is the voice of the vast majority of the Trade Unions in the country.

Unison
http://www.unison.org.uk/

The UNISON web-site is built by their own communications team, and they have built an interesting site which even includes a screen-saver for your own use! There is a note on the pages saying that the site is always under construction and expansion and advance apologies for any links which don't work. Their warning is needed, a large number of the pages when tested weren't available, but hopefully this is a matter which will receive attention over the coming months.

Politics on the Net Abroad

Politics on the Internet in the UK is fairly well progressed, much further than most other large countries, with the exception of the US. All this talk of an information super-highway was started by a US politician, and most of the set-up of the Internet was started by various US servers linking the military institutions together.

This section does not pretend to be exhaustive. There are so many foreign political sites it is almost impossible to mention them all. We have covered some of the English speaking countries in more detail as well as provided some of the better 'links' sites to foreign political parties, governments and world leaders.

The United States

An interesting situation is that the UK is around two years behind the US in terms of Internet technology and content. If nothing else this allows us to see the way that we can expect our own country's web-sites to develop by looking at the current US situation. If we do follow this course, then things look very promising. Like the UK, there has been a period when politicians were sceptical of this new medium, but more and more are getting used to it, and more and more information is coming on-line.

Some sites of interest to those wanting to see the on-line "sites" of the American political system are:

CAMPAIGN 2000

Al Gore for President
http://www.algore2000.com

Alan Keyes for President

http://www.keyes2000.org/

Bill Bradley for President
http:///www.billbradley.com

Bob Dornan for President
http://www.angelfire.com/il/Dornan/

Bob Smith for President
http://www.smithforpresident.org/

Bushwatch!
http://www.geocities.com/CapitolHill/3750/bush.htm

Candidate Links Page
http://www.niu.edu/newsplace/wh4.html#4a

Election2000 Watch
http://home.pacbell.net/nmasters/2000.htm

Elizabeth Dole for President
http://www.e-dole2000.org/

Gary Bauer for President
http://www.bauer2k.com/

George W Bush for President (unofficial)
http://www.geocities.com/CapitolHill/Senate/4124/

George W Bush for President (exploratory)
http://www.georgewbush.com/

GW Bush Satire Site
http://www.gwbush.com/

John Kasich for President
http://www.2000gop.com/kasich/

Orrin Hatch for President
http://www.orrinhatch.org/

Pat Buchanan for President
http://www.gopatgo2000.com

Steve Forbes for President
http://www.forbes2000.com/

White House 2000
http://www.niu.edu/newsplace/whitehouse.html

Presidential Election Site
http://www.lib.virginia.edu/gic/elections/index.html

US GOVERNMENT

Links to Departments of Government
http://www.whitehouse.gov/WH/Cabinet/html/cabinet_links.html

Links to State/Local Governments
http://lcweb.loc.gov/global/state/stategov.html

House of Representatives
http://www.house.gov

Senate
http://www.senate.gov

White House
http://www.whitehouse.gov

US GENERAL POLITICAL SITES

Democratic National Committee

http://www.democrats.org/index.html

Eisenhower Centre
http://www.history.cc.ukans.edu/heritage/abilene/ikectr.html/

Political Graveyard: Political Burial Sites
http://www.potifos.com/tpg/index.html/

Presidential Election Site
http://www.lib.virginia.edu/gie/elections/index.html/

Presidential Speech Archive
http://www.tame.edu/scom/pres/archive.html/

Republican National Committee
http://www.rnc.org/

Richard Nixon Presidential Library
http://www.nixonfoundation.org/

Southern Politics Site
http://members.aol.com/thecitadel/sopol/

Watergate Site
http://www.washingtonpost.com/wpsrv/national/longterm/watergate/frot.htm

Ireland

Fianna Fail
http://www.fiannafail.ie/index.html

Fine Gael
http://www.finegael.com/

Government of Ireland Website
http://www.irlgov.ie/

Irish Political & Government Links
http://www.niceone.com/gov.htm

Labour Party
http://www.labour.ie/

Sinn Fein
http://sinnfein.ie/index.html

Australia

Australian Democrats
http://www.democrats.org.au

Australian Elections Homepage
http://mullara.met.unimelb.edu.au:8080/home/blah/elections/elections.html

Australian Parliament
http://www.aph.gov.au/

Australian Political Resources
http://wwwplato.itsc.adfa.edu.au/apt/

Federal Government Homepage
http://www.fed.gov.au

Labor Party
http://www.alp.org.au

Liberal Party
http://www.liberal.org.au

National Party
http://www.ozemail.com.au/~npafed/

One Nation
http://www.onenation.com.au

Paul Keating Homepage
http://www.keating.org.au/home.html

Political Science in Australia
http://www.anu.edu.au/polsci/austpol/

Prime Minister's Homepage
http://www.pm.gov.au

State & Local Government Links
http://wwwgwb.com.au/gwh/com/comm4.html

CANADA

Bloc Quebecois
http://www.blocquebecois.parl.gc.ca/accueil.htm

Canadian Election Information
http://polisci.nelson.com/elections.html

Canadian Parliament
http://www.parl.gc.ca/index.html

Canadian Political Links
http://www.clo.com/~canadainfo/gov.html

Elections Canada
http://www.elections.ca/

Government of Canada
http://canada.gc.ca/

Liberal Party
http://www.liberal.ca/

New Democratic Party
http://www.ndp.ca/

Provincial Government Links
http://www.infocan.gc.ca/p-link.html

NEW ZEALAND

ACT Party
http://www.act.org.nz/

Alliance Party
http://www.alliance.org.nz/

Labour Party
http://www.labour.org.nz/

National Party
http://www.national.org.nz/

New Zealand First Party
http://www.nzforst.org.nz/

New Zealand Government
http://www.govt.nz/

New Zealand Electoral Agencies
http://www.elections.org.nz/elections/index.html

New Zealand Government
http://www.executive.govt.nz/

New Zealand Parliament
http://parliament.govt.nz/

SOUTH AFRICA

African National Congress
http://www.anc.org.za/

Parliament
http://www.parliament.gov.za/

South African Government Information
http://www.gov.za

South African Parliament Site

http://polity.org.za/govdocs/parliament/index.html

EUROPEAN NATIONAL PARLIAMENTS' HOME-PAGES

Albania
http://www.parliament.tirana.al/

Austria
http://www.parliament.gv.at/

Belgian Lower House
http://www.lachambre.be/

Belgian Senate
http://www.fed-parl.be/

Denmark (Folketing)
http://www.folktinget.dk/

Finland (Eduskunta)
http://www.eduskunta.fi/

France (Assemblee Nationale)
http://www.assemblee-nat.fr

France (Senate)
http://www.senat.fr

Germany (Bundestag)
http://http:www.bundesregierung.de/

Ireland (Dail)
http://www.irlgov.ie

Italy (House of Deputies)
http://www.parlamento.it/

Luxemburg (House of Deputies)
http://www.chd.lu

Netherlands
http://www.parlement.nl/

Spain (Congress of Deputies)
http://www.congresso.es

Spain (Senate)
http://www.senado.es

Sweden (Riksdagen)
http://riksdagen.se

EUROPEAN POLITICAL SITES

European Elections Online
http://www.fes.de/election/

European Elections Site
http://www.agora.stm.it/elections/elections/europeanunion.htm

European Elections Studies
http://www.uh.edu/~mfrankl2/EES.html

European Political Parties & Youth Organisations
http://home.luna.nl/~benne/pp/eur/index.htm

Poltical Resources in the EU
http://www.europointcom.co.uk/PREU/index2.html

Austrian Political Links
http://www.europointcom.co.uk/PREU/austria.html

Belgian Political Links
http://www.europointcom.co.uk/PREU/belgium.html

Danish Political Links
http://www.europointcom.co.uk/PREU/denmark.html

Dutch Political Links
http://www.europointcom.co.uk/PREU/netherlands.html

Finnish Political Links
http://www.europointcom.co.uk/PREU/finland.html

French Political Links

http://www.europointcom.co.uk/PREU/france.html

German Political Links

http://www.europointcom.co.uk/PREU/germany.html

Greek Political Links

http://www.europointcom.co.uk/PREU/greece.html

Irish Political Links

http://www.europointcom.co.uk/PREU/ireland.html

Italian Political Links

http://www.europointcom.co.uk/PREU/italy.html

Luxemburg Political Links

http://www.europointcom.co.uk/PREU/luxembourg.html

Portuguese Political Links

http://www.europointcom.co.uk/PREU/portugal.html

Spanish Political Links

http://www.europointcom.co.uk/PREU/spain.html

Swedish Political Links

http://www.europointcom.co.uk/PREU/sweden.html

WORLD POLITICAL SITES

Elections Around the World
http://www.agora.stm.h/elections/election/main.htm

Elections Calendar
http://www.agora.stm.h/elections/calendar.htm

Electoral Studies Website
http://www.psci.unt.edu/es/

Governments & Parliaments
http://www.worldlib.org/parliaments.html

Governments & Related Organisations
http://www.moe.edu.sg/schools/saje/intgov.htm

Heads of State & Ministers
http://www.odci.gov/cia/publications/chiefs/chiefs-toc-view.html

Parliaments Around the World
http://agora.stm.it/elections/parties.htm

Parliaments on the Web
http://www.ipu.org/english/parlweb.htm

Political Leaders' Websites
http://www.udayton.edu/~polsci/group3.htm

Political Parties Around the World
http://www.agora.stm.it/elections/parties.htm

Political Parties of the World
http://www.gksoft.com/govt/en/parties.html

Women in Politics
http://www.netsrq.com/~dbois/govern.html

World Government Links
http://www.gksoft.com/govt/en/

World Leaders Email Addresses
http://www.trytel.com/~aberdeen/
World Political Leaders 1945-98

http://web.jet.es/ziaorarr/00index.htm

World Rulers Site
http://www.geocities.com/Athens/1058/rulers.html

INTERNATIONAL ORGANISATIONS

Commonwealth Parliamentary Association
http://comparlhq.org.uk/frames.htm/

Council of Europe
http://stars.coe.fr/

European Union
http://europe.eu.int/index.htm

G-8
http://www.g7.utoronto.ca/

International Labour Organisation
http://www.ilo.org/

International Monetary Fund
http://www.imf.org/

NATO
http://www.nato.int/home.htm

OECD
http://www.oecd.org/

Organisation of American States
http://www.oas.org/

UNESCO
http://www.unesco.org/

United Nations
http://www.un.org/

World Bank
http://www.worldbank.org/

World Health Organisation
http://www.who.int/

World Trade Organisation
http://www.wto.org/

Political Party Web-Sites

All the major political parties now have web-sites, although they are used in different ways and to different levels. Below you can find all the main political party web-sites, as well as the range of sites from the branches.

It is worth looking back at how the political party sites developed. Initially, back in 1995, they were really only used at the Party Conference to promote the ideas that were being circulated there. The Liberal Democrats had used compuserve a lot for internal communications, and appeared to have a strategy for their on-line presence. By 1996 it was clear that the Internet was inevitably going to play a more important part in party politics, as every major party had gone on-line and increased the scope of its presence.

Parties started to use the Internet as both part of their advertising strategy, as well as a press release information area and included pages so that people could find out how to join. Providing information to members was important, and all the web-sites developed password areas for members to get graphics for their leaflets and further information about the progress in the party.

All three of the main political parties have used, albeit on a small-scale, their web-sites to sell party goods. On offer on the Labour site have been tea-towels, whilst the Tories have previously featured puzzles of John and Norma Major, whilst the Liberal Democrats have sold mugs. Not exactly what one might call the most informative content possible, but still an interesting marketing exercise, which it seems has had at least some success.

The Internet is still used very little in most constituencies, and given that there are 659 constituencies, there should be many more web-sites around. The number is increasing slowly, but many of the sites are plagued by the perennial Internet problem, initial enthusiasm which soon dies down. Some sites have events which are over 6 months out-of-date, and numerous Conservative Associations still have their events from before the General Election listed as their most recent. Such web-pages are better taken down than left up.

However, the trend is that more and more Associations are getting themselves an on-line presence and putting considerable effort into it. As more and more regional groups have trouble recruiting, it is likely that more and more will put time and effort into creating and maintaining their web-sites when they realise they could attract even more valuable members.

CONSERVATIVE PARTY

Official Conservative Party Web-Site
http://www.conservative-party.org.uk/
Youth Web-site
http://www.conservative-party.org.uk/future/

The official party web-site is not what one might call fast, it takes a long time for the graphically intensive site to load, but you are treated to a picture of William Hague slowly appearing on the screen. The navigation is simple, albeit slightly tardy, and there are contact details for each of the main party organisations.

The Conservatives were the last major political party to enter the on-line political realm, and their site contains all the basic information that you would expect, but little more. The youth web-site did have its own domain name, but in mid-1999 it disappeared to be replaced with a web-page from the main party site.

In 1998, Conservative Future was set up to replace with one body the old three bodies of the Young Conservatives, Conservative Students and Conservative Graduates. The new Chairman Donal Blaney organised a domain name, but didn't create a site, and after a year a short page on the main Conservative Party was made available with contact details for the organisation.

TOP THREE TORY CONSTITUENCY SITES

Basildon

http://www.netlink.co.uk/users/horgan/bascon

This site, run by Stephen Horgan, provides an up-to-date analysis of what is happening in the constituency, and also contains articles written by local members.

Guildford

http://www.guildfordconservatives.org/

Guildford Conservative's web-site is a site which is kept up-to-date, and contains information about the youth section of the party, press releases, local events as well as comments and speeches from the local Conservative MP. Minor flaws aside, a lot of effort has gone into the site, and it is certainly a site which other constituencies should be trying to recreate.

North West Hampshire

http://www.nwh-tories.org.uk/

Although this site was a few months out-of-date at time of writing, it is a relatively large site, with local links, election results, press releases and general information about the local constituency. The local Conservative MP, Sir George Young, also has his own web-site at *http://www.sir-george-young.org.uk/* and their are well-sited links between the two. Sir George and his local constituency have both worked well together to provides sites which are useful and informative for both constituents and general visitors to the site.

TOP THREE TORY STUDENT SITES

Keele University

http://www.keele.ac.uk/socs/ks20/

I haven't been biased by including this site. It is more than two years since I stopped running the site, so I can claim independence from it now. The site from Keele Conservative Future is well presented and does the job it's intended to do.

Warwick University
http://www.csv.warwick.ac.uk/~suaba

Formerly run by Ivor Peksa, this site no longer contains the useful information provided by him (now at *http://www.club.demon.co.uk*), but they are a well-built set of pages.

York University
http://www.york.ac.uk/~socs35

York University's Conservative site is well-known. Or it was back in 1995 when a hacker broke into the site and kindly uploaded porn and abuse. The number of accesses to the site rocketed (potential one might think for the main Conservative Central Office site?) until Central Office took drastic action. The site today links to generally useful sources of information and resources on the Internet.

LABOUR PARTY

Official Party Web-Site
http://www.labour.org.uk/
Youth Party Web-Site
http://www.poptel.org.uk/regeneration

The Labour site was first set up in 1994, the second main political party to do so. Labour's web-site is quite a slow affair, which is very short on information. Apart from the basic "how to join" and details of who the leaders of the party are, there is little else currently on the site. There are only four news releases, although there are short biographies of all of the Cabinet Ministers. During the General Election of 1997 Labour's site was full of useful information and played a major role in their campaign. Since then it has been allowed to slip, with much of the information being taken off. However, we understand that a major relaunch is about to happen.

TOP THREE LABOUR CONSTITUENCY SITES

Carlisle
http://www.geocities.com/CapitolHill/Senate/3524/

This site contains the local election results, information about the local politicians and about the Association.

Southampton
http://www.users.globalnet.co.uk/~harrier/

A very nicely presented site which covers the two Labour held seats in Southampton. The site allows users to report any problems they might need help with in the council, and there is information about the two local Labour MPs

Wythenshawe & Sale East
http://www.geocities.com/CapitolHill/1374/

The site contains brief details about the local constituency and the MP, as well as detailing the local council boundaries.

TOP THREE LABOUR STUDENT SITES

Bath University
http://www.bath.ac.uk/~su2lsa/home.html

Although short on information, this site currently has information about the labour club, and is kept up-to-date with the latest events which they are planning to hold.

Edinburgh University
http://www.ed.ac.uk/~labour

A nice slick site which although short of information, remembers that students at the university want to know information such as how to join and where to go to attend the meetings. A large committee reflects the size of this Association.

York University
http://www-users.york.ac.uk/~socs138/main-index.html

This site wins the prize for the strangest colour scheme of any political web-site currently in circulation at the moment with buttons that could well generate a headache for the slightly more sensitive. Underneath this exterior are a range of pages covering the work and aims of the club.

LIBERAL DEMOCRATS

Official Party Web-Site
http://www.libdems.org.uk/
Scottish Liberal Democrats
http://www.scotlibdems.co.uk/

Compared to the relatively low standards set by the Conservative Party and the Labour Party this is substantially better. The Liberal Democrat web-page has a range of press releases and party information, as well as detailed biographies of all of its MPs. Certain parts of the site are under construction, and have been for some time, Although not as good as it could potentially be, this web-site is probably the best of the main political parties.

TOP THREE LIBERAL DEMOCRAT CONSTITUENCY SITES

Web-sites always become out-of-date, and there are more than a few Liberal Democrat associations that have out-of-date web-sites. It is disappointing to see that so many constituencies have made the effort to go on-line, but have then neglected their presence. In the case of the Liberal Democrats I know of 12 non-student sites which haven't been updated in the last 15 months or longer.

Like Essex Liberal Democrats, who are mentioned below, it might be worthwhile for Associations of all political parties to join together in one block to create their web-sites, rather than risking going it alone and being unable to keep the site up-to-date. Three good exceptions to this rule are:

Aylesbury
http://www.compulink.co.uk/~broadway/ald.html

Although it says on this site that it will be removed in mid-1998, it is still present a year later. At the time of the last General Election it was a very useful resource about the local party, but unfortunately it hasn't been updated since and shows how unimpressive this type of out-of-date site can become.

St Albans
http://www.stalbanslibdems.org.uk/

One of the few Liberal Democrat associations with its own domain name, this is a short and concise site, but has a range of information on how to join and the activities of those involved.

Essex Liberal Democrats
http://www.essex.libdems.org/

Although this is more of a regional site, it is kept up-to-date, and has information on a number of constituencies. It is a well presented site with a range of up-to-date news releases and contains links to a large range of official Liberal Democrats sites and information.

Top Three Liberal Democrat Student Sites

Cardiff University Liberal Democrats
http://www.cf.ac.uk/uwcc/suon/libdems/

Cardiff University LibDems have an animated graphic which shortens the messages of the party to, "Building for the Long-Term", "Investing in People" and "Drinking Lots of Beer". The site is slightly out-of-date, but at least has some humour. They claim that one of the reasons to join the Liberal Democrats is to "get a nice golden glow whenever Paddy comes on the telly...". Some would argue that they get a different feeling whenever Paddy comes on the telly.....

Durham University Liberal Democrats
http://www.dur.ac.uk/~dds8lda/start.html

Although this site is slightly out-of-date, it contains details of the meetings and events held by the Association, and gives details of how to join. It is a well-designed site, despite being relatively small.

Edinburgh University Liberal Democrats
http://www.ed.ac.uk/~libdems

This was one of the better sites, but it hasn't been updated since early 1998, so I will await developments.

SCOTTISH NATIONAL PARTY (SNP)

Official Party Web-Site
http://www.snp.org.uk/
Youth Part Web-Site
http://www.architist.freeserve.co.uk/

There are a small, but steadily increasing, number of sites by the different branches of the SNP. South Ayr has a site at *http://www.southayr.demon.co.uk/* which includes a brief history of the SNP as well as other information about the SNP both in Ayr and in Scotland generally. Rather surprisingly the other largish web-site about the SNP is from the London branch at *http://scottalk.net/londonsnp/*. Although not recently updated, the SNP group in Edinburgh East have a web-site at http://www.dishon.freeserve.co.uk/snp/ which includes their local party newspaper on-line.

The Youth organisation has a web-site at *http://www.architist .freeserve.co.uk/* which links to all of the Party's student sites, mostly at universities. Of these, probably the best at the moment is that of Aberdeen University at *http://www.abdn.ac.uk/~src121/*.

PLAID CYMRU

Official Party Web Site
http://www.plaid-cymru.wales.com/

This site contains, in both English and Welsh of course, a range of information about the party, as well as details of candidates at upcoming elections and the latest version of their manifesto.

A selection of branches of Plaid Cymru now have their own sites, including Ceredigion which has a information packed site at *http://ourworld.compuserve.com/homepages/PlaidCymruCeredigion/*, but which has become slightly out-of-date. For younger members of the party, the Federation of Plaid Cymru has a site at *http://www.btinternet.com/~ws/plaid/index-s.html*, which also has details of events and meetings in Aberystwyth.

NORTHERN IRELAND POLITICAL PARTIES

For sake of political independence on this matter, I have listed the websites of all those political parties that take part in Northern Ireland politics.

One of the most well-known political parties is *Sinn Fein, http://www.irlnet.com/sinnfein/*. The site contains a range of useful information about the party. The site moves from time to time usually on the free accounts provided by the Geocities (*http://www.geocities.com/*). Some of the split-off parties from Sinn Fein develop their own web-sites, sometimes for informational purposes, on other occasions for fund-raising reasons. Republican Sinn Fein also have a web-site, which again is sometimes unavailable, at *http://indigo.ie/~saoirse/record.htm*.

The Ulster Unionists have a web-site at *http://www.uup.org/*. There are a range of unionist parties in addition to the Ulster Unionist Party which are on-line, such as the Ulster Democratic Party, *http://www.udp.org/*, and the Ulster Democratic Unionist Party, *http://www.dup.org.uk/*.

The Alliance Party at *http://www.allianceparty.org/* used to be written and maintained by Nicholas Whyte, and it became a substantial resource on elections and politics in Northern Ireland. The site now contains information about the party, which is the sister party of the Liberal Democrats, and a range of speeches and publications.

Nicholas Whyte's new web-site about Northern Irish politics can be found at *http://explorers.whyte.com/*. Although it may not win awards for graphical presentation, it contains some of the most useful electoral information about Northern Ireland available, and it has links to a large number of similar resources which are available elsewhere.

If you want a list of political web-sites span both Northern Ireland and the Republic of Ireland, then visit *http://www.ukpol.co.uk/irish.htm*, which has a wide range of links to various institutions and groups. The Northern Ireland Office Internet site also often updates on the situation in Northern Ireland, and the state of the political parties. The main page of this can be found at *http://www.nics.gov.uk/*.

SPIN-OFF PARTIES

Every major UK political party has spin-offs of some variety, the Labour Party have organisations such as the Socialist Workers party, the Conservatives have the pro-European Conservative Party, and the Liberal Democrats have the Liberal Party. I have listed these parties below by category of political party.

LABOUR PARTY

New Labour was very different to Old Labour in terms of the member-ship, many of the left-wing elements in the party felt uncomfortable. A large number of socialist web-sites were placed on-line, although in terms of the quality and speed, they are relatively slow to grasp the technology available. The large number of parties that split are now though starting to gain web-sites, and the confusion continues on-line. The following have web-sites.

The Socialist Equality Party (*http://dialspace.dial.pipex.com/sep/*), the Socialist Labour Party (*http://www.ifley.demon.co.uk/index.html*), the Socialist Party (*http://www.socialistparty.org.uk/*), the Socialist Party of Great Britain (*http://ourworld.compuserve.com/homepages/worldsm/spgb.htm*) and the Socialist Worker's Party (*http://ourworld.compuserve.com/homepages/SWP_Britain*).

CONSERVATIVE PARTY

When William Hague became leader of the Conservative Party, he immediately banned or restricted some of the political groupings which he felt had plagued, and eventually brought down, the previous

Conservative Government. This meant that a range of the web-sites available at this time suddenly disappeared, and there aren't (to my knowledge) any spin-offs to the party which have web-pages.

LIBERAL DEMOCRATS

The Liberal Democrats found themselves in what some might call political turmoil in the 1980s, before they were re-united as a common party by Paddy Ashdown. However, when the SDP and the Liberal Alliance merged, some members didn't feel comfortable, and the Liberal Party was formed (or continued). This has proved more successful than many might realise the party has Councillors and does relatively well in General Elections. The site can be found at *http://www.libparty. demon.co.uk/*, and is maintained by the Liberal Councillor Nigel Ashford.

* * *

There are a host of other political parties which exist in this country. The Internet makes it quite difficult to find out whether these are one-man bands who have set up their own web-site to further their political beliefs, or whether they're serious political groups which want to make an electoral impression. With some of the other parties, such as the Monster Raving Loony Party, it's not entirely obvious what the point is! But they continue to liven up British politics in by-elections, even after the sad death of their leader, Screaming Lord Sutch, in 1999.

It is a shame that the Monster Raving Loony Party Web-Site doesn't appear to have functioned since the 1997 General Election, it often provided a sobering view of political life. But not to worry, the party of yogic flying is still around, the Natural Law Party has a web-site at *http://www .natural-law-party.org.uk/*.

There are a range of anti-Monarchy parties which have been set up, usually on a free US server such as Geocities. An example is the British Republican party which can be found at *http://www.geocities.com /CapitolHill/Parliament/2392/index.html* and the web-site of the Movement Against the Monarchy which is at *http://www.geocities. com/CapitolHill/Lobby/1793/Index.html*. Beware though, even by their own admission, they do not put their point across in diplomatic and succinct language.

107

A web-site based on a simple principle is entitled Class War, and can be found at *http://www.geocities.com/CapitolHill/9482/*. It is interesting to see that a large number of political information and pressure groups sites can be found at Geocities, so visiting *http://www.geocities.com/search/* and typing in a few relevant search words related to your political interest might yield some interesting results.

There are also some parties such as the Albion Party, *http://www.geocities.com/capitolhill/8214/index.htm*, whose web-site is not always available. A similar sort of site is the Whig Party, http://home.clara.net/gamestheory/whigs.html. With sites such as these, it's never immediately obvious what the intent of the party is, to gain political power in local Government, gain political power in national Government, or just to have fun.

The final word on political party web-sites goes to the British Democratic Dictatorship Party at *http://come.to/bddp*. Despite the party name which is arguably a contradiction, the web-site lays out some of the policies which the party leader, Dr Richard Turner, believes in. Before you get to these policies you are faced with a button which declares that the party is the fasting growing in Britain. The party believes in capital punishment in public, which will be held at Wembley each year in front of a massive audience who will have each paid ten pounds to watch the spectacle. The solution to the Israeli and Iraqi problems is to give the Iraqi land to Yasser Arafat.

Analysis

We often hear claims about how interested a political party is in the Internet. Below are some figures which show exactly which parties can claim to be the real party of IT. By measuring the number of branches of the party on-line, the number of constituencies, the number of MPs, Councillors and MEPs with e-mail, we get the results below. The figures below relate only to those e-mail addresses and web-pages that we know about. The Councillors e-mail figures relate to the number of Councillor's e-mail addresses that I have been informed about over the last four years. It is intended to give a guide-line only in this instance, and the figures for all three parties are almost certainly substantially higher.

Number of Branches (Associations and Students) On-Line

Conservative Party	31
Labour Party	17
Liberal Democrats	15

Number of Councillors With E-Mail Addresses

Conservative Party	141
Labour Party	179
Liberal Democrats	318

Number of MPs With E-Mail Addresses

Conservative Party	9/162	5.6%
Labour Party	35/415	8.43
Liberal Democrats	36/46	78.2

The winning party, by a substantial distance, who can really claim (at the moment at least) to be the most "wired" political party are therefore the Liberal Democrats.

THE CONTRIBUTION OF THE POLITICIANS

One of the earliest politician to show an on-line presence was the Labour MP for Cambridge, Anne Campbell. She not only was contactable by e-mail, but she had a web-page, and she had a on-line surgery from time to time. Given her constituency, which contained a large number of youngsters and students and professionals who had Internet access, this was almost inevitable, but she can claim to be one the pioneers. Her site is *http://www.worldserver.pipex.com/anne.campbell/*.

Other Labour MPs to have their own web-page now include David Blunkett, who has his own site at *http://www.home.co.uk/dblunkettmp/* which has a collection of speeches Blunkett has made, as well as policy statements and his own CV. Given his current position in Government as Secretary of State for Education and Employment, there are several spelling mistakes on the site which are unfortunate.

In terms of content, the Labour MP for the City of Durham, Gerry Steinberg, has a web-site at *http://www.users.zetnet.co.uk/pcrrn/steinberg/*, which provides valuable information, such as the local election results for the constituency, information about joining the party locally, as well as some information on him personally, including a selection of his speeches. He has also collected links about his local area, which many MPs haven't done, but which provide a valuable addition to sites such as these.

Some Members of Parliament may sometimes feel that the Internet is doing them no favours. There were a series of false allegations made against the Labour MP for Newark, Fiona Jones. Cleared of electoral fraud by the courts, some web-sites were not so quick to restore her good name. Fiona Jones herself though has battled on, and is not only contactable by e-mail, but also has a well-designed and informative web-site at *http://www.business.u-net.com/~newlab*.

Some sites aren't always kept up-to-date, the Labour MP for Loughborough, Andy Reed admits on his site that "this page is now three years out-of-date and in desperate need of updating". The previous site was relatively comprehensive, and the new-site at *http://www.poptel .org.uk/andrew.reed/* promises to be much bigger and better still, so hopefully this will turn out to be one of the better Labour Party web-sites.

Conservative politicians haven't always been the first to dip their feet into the virtual world, but many of the MPs did make an effort. David Shaw, the former MP for Dover, contributed to the political news-groups, as well as having a web-page and being contactable by e-mail. He was one of the Conservatives MPs who made some of the more noticeable appearances generally, and his site offered prizes for those who could answer various partisan political questions.

Another MP who has long had e-mail, and indeed was a Cabinet Minister at the time, is Sir George Young, who has a site at *http://www.sir-george-young.org.uk/*. This site is very large and kept very up-to-date with a large number of articles about Sir George and his thoughts. Small parts of the site are still under construction, but since it is linked in with his own constituency web-site at *http://www.nwh-tories.org.uk/*, this is an immensely impressive effort.

There are still not all that many Conservative MPs with web-sites, and the number really should be higher, but an increasing number are making an effort. Angela Browning has a site at *http://www.abrowning .demon.co.uk/*, and although it might not win any prizes for design, it is kept up-to-date with various press releases, and gives interesting comments and contact details about Angela Browning.

One of the better Conservative MPs' web-sites belongs to Geoffrey Clifton-Brown, and can be found at *http://www.gcbmp.demon.co.uk/*. It may not be an enormous site, but it contains press releases, MP information, constituency information, all of which are items which we should expect from more and more MPs. By including his recent speeches in the House of Commons, he is at least telling his constituents what he is doing on their behalf.

One of the few MPs with his own domain name is Tim Collins, whose site can be found at *http://www.timcollins.co.uk/*, and the site is well-presented and interesting. There is a short "frequently answered questions" guide, which will hopefully turn into an extremely useful first point of reference for visitors to any MP's web-site. Also included is a useful diary of events in the Houses of Parliament that the MP thinks his constituents would be interested in. A very worth-while web-site.

Michael Fabricant, the Conservative MP for Lichfield, has a web-site at *http://www.solnet.co.uk/fabricant/*, which has an entire sub-page containing nothing but pictures of Michael Fabricant. You can see Michael in a hospital with his shirt undone, you can see Michael in the Arctic Circle with the Royal Marines, Michael with a young female constituent on each arm, Michael in a nursery school, and, oh, you get the idea. If you are designing a web-site and happen to need a picture of Michael Fabricant, then this site is ideal. The site is actually very well-designed, and also has a number of press releases and information which is kept up-to-date and is of genuine interest to his constituents.

Paddy Ashdown claimed in 1995 that his party was the most wired of them all. From the number of their MPs with e-mail addresses, and the number of activists on-line, this was a claim that did seem at least partly based on reality. Paddy Ashdown did have an e-mail address, although it was claimed that he never actually read it himself. From personal experience, I did get a response from his e-mail address many years ago, although whether the great man himself replied I'll never know.

The Liberal Democrats have a much better web-site where all of their MPs, albeit it a smaller number, have a web-page with information about them in some detail. Although there aren't links to their speeches and so on from these pages, which is hopefully something which will be added in the future, it does provide an interesting starting point for those wanting to find out more.

Some MPs also have some small web-sites, which is still more than creditable, as it least gives an initial point of contact for constituents. One of these is run by Stephen Day, the Conservative MP for Cheadle, whose web-site can be found at *http://www.users.zetnet.co.uk/cheadle-day/*. Angela Eagle, the Labour MP, also has a relatively small web-site at *http://www.poptel.org.uk/angela.eagle.mp/*, but it provides information on some of the speeches she has made, including her maiden speech, and other various information about the constituency.

Although every Liberal Democrat MP has an e-mail address, few of them have web-sites. One of these is Vincent Cable, the MP for Twickenham. The web-site at *http://www.compulink.co.uk/~icph/cablewin.htm*, is just a basic web-page about him, and doesn't contain much further information about his speeches or other work, although it does provide comprehensive contact information.

Nigel Evans, the Conservative MP for the Ribble Valley is another MP who has had an on-line presence for a considerable time. This site is well worth visiting, if only for the picture of Nigel Evans which has been edited to reshape his head. His site can be found at *http://www .nigelmp.com/* and contains other useful information about the constituency. Eleanor Laing, the Conservative MP for Epping Forest has a web-site at *http://www.efca.demon.co.uk/*, but unfortunately it hasn't been updated since the 1997 General Election.

So the conclusion from the web-sites currently available is that the Conservative MPs have produced the better web-sites and have produced more of them in percentage terms than any of the other two main parties. However, these things can always change, and I can well imagine that in ten years time there will be very few MPs who don't have a web-site with at least basic information about themselves on it.

Charities and Pressure Groups

There are many charities and groups in this country who seek to influence Government policy, and although they have widely different funding levels and targets, many are very successful with their campaigns. Many don't have web-sites, many have weak web-sites but some have very good on-line presences, and these are looked at over the next few pages.

Environmental groups use the Internet probably more than any other distinct type of pressure group except possibly the anti-European Union brigade. There are always details of conferences being re-laid around the Internet, and there are an immense range of environmental resources for anyone interested in finding out more about the major issues.

The Friends of the Earth, *http://www.foe.co.uk/*, are one of the most influential of the groups and one of the leading on-line players. Within their web-site, there are frequent updates of their campaigns, such as the infamous Newbury Bypass Campaign, *http://www.foe.co.uk/action/ newbury*. Friends of the Earth in Scotland have their own web-site at *http://www.foe-scotland.org.uk/*.

The other large environmental pressure group is Greenpeace, *http://www.greenpeace.org.uk/*, who have a site which covers the problems which they perceive to be world-wide. Despite the mistakes some commentators claim that Greenpeace made over the Shell Oil Rig in the North Sea, they remain one of the most respected pressure groups, and are a first point of reference on the Internet.

In 1999, a group of over one hundred Greenpeace supporters set up the web-site of Sane BP or "BP Share-holders against new oil exploration" at *http://www.sanebp.com/*. An interesting feature at this site is an on-line calculator called the Corporate Sanity Calculator which shows you how much the business spends on oil exploration as compared to how much is invested into renewable energy.

Roads have been a major political issue over the last few years, and the Newbury Bypass Campaign has already been mentioned. In addition, there has been the Third Battle of Newbury Web-Site with additional information about the "battle" which took place, and this can be found at *http://www.gn.apc.org/newbury/*.

There are a number of web-sites related to anti-hunting matters on resources such as Geocities, but these are often short-lived sites which are soon forgotten and soon deleted. A useful site which is packed with resources is the Hunt Saboteur's Association at *http://envirolink.org/arrs /HSA/hsa.html*, which is a well designed site furthering the cause of animal rights.

Other sites of interest are the Green Network, *http://www.solnet.co .uk/green-network/*, and the English Nature (albeit it a Government linked site, not a pressure group) at *http://www.english-nature.org.uk/*, and also the Naturenet site at *http://www.naturenet.net*.

The Green Party throughout Europe have a lot of their members on-line, and there is a specific UK discussion group on USENET called uk.politics.environment, where a lot of the press releases from the above organisations are propagated by supporters.

There are an ever-increasing number of web-sites which are there to campaign against Britain's membership of the European Union. One of the better ones is called Eurocritic, and can be found at *http://www.eurocritic.demon.co.uk/*. This also contains the web-site of Business For Sterling at *http://www.eurocritic.demon.co.uk/bfspress.htm* as well as being the home-page of the Bruges Group, of which more information can be found at *http://www.eurocritic.demon.co.uk/about-bg.htm*.

The Campaign Against Euro-Federalism has a web-site at *http://www. poptel.org.uk/against-eurofederalism/*, which has a range of interesting articles which promote their cause. Although inevitably biased given the subject matter, there are some interesting historic pages, one of which is about the military history of the EU can be found at *http://www.poptel.org.uk/against-eurofederalism/weu.html*.

Charter 88 at *http://www.charter88.org.uk/* have a superb web-site, the aim of the group is to educate and inform people of matters related to reform of the democratic system, and they support such measures as ending the first-past-the-post system, providing a powerful Freedom of Information Act and generally making Parliament more accessible. The web-site has details of the groups aims, and provides resources which support the group's campaigns. The site is easy to navigate and has won a place in this directory's top ten political web-sites.

Top-Ten

A directory like this wouldn't be complete without at least some subjective rating of what the top ten web-sites are on the Internet. So below is a list which I consider to be the top ten UK political sites on the Internet, but for those not listed, there's always time for some promotions for the next edition.

1	Monarchy Web-Site	*http://www.royal.gov.uk/*
2	The FCO	*http://www.fco.gov.uk/*
3	New Deal	*http://www.newdeal.gov.uk/*
4	Birmingham Council	*http://www.birmingham.gov.uk/*
5	Local Government	*http://www.oultwood.com/localgov/*
6	Nicholas Whyte	*http://explorers.whyte.com/*
7	Charter 88	*http://www.charter88.org.uk/*
8	Adopt an MP	*http://www.stand.org.uk/*
9	Centre For Reform	*http://www.cfr.org.uk/*
10	Republic	*http://www.republic.org/*

The Monarchy web-site is simply first-class, providing information at a range of different levels, which will appeal to all audiences. The Foreign and Commonwealth Office have led the way forward for Government Departments for a number of years, and with options to personalise your front page, and more besides, this is a site that is of genuine interest to all those going abroad, not just those wishing to read the department's press releases. All of the other sites are worth a mention and have featured in the above directory for good reason.

Over the next year I hope that all of these sites continue to develop an improve, to remain the trail-blazing sites which they currently are.

My humble congratulations to them all.

The Definitive List

Please note that all sites in our list were checked numerous occasions before the book went to print to check they were all available. Some sites were removed from the list if they were unavailable when we checked on them, and some were removed if they contained no content.

Abelard.org
http://www.abelard.org/ (Web-Page)
http://www.abelard.org/emu/emu-hi.htm (Why EMU is bad)

Aberdeen, Earl (former PM)
http://www.ukpol.co.uk/biooo.htm

Aberdeenshire (council)
http://www.aberdeenshire.gov/govhome.htm (Council Information)
http://www.aberdeenshire.goc.uk (Web-Page)

ACAS (See Advisory, Concilliation and Arbitration Service)

Access to the Countryside Bill
http://www.parlaiment.the-stationery-office.co.uk/pa/cm199798/cmbills/054/1997054.

Accounts Commision For Scotland
http://www.scot-ac.gov.uk/ (Web-Page)

Adam Smith Institute
http://www.adamsmith.org.uk/policy/bulletin/b23htm (Adam Smith Bulletin)
http://www.adamsmithinstitute.com/ (International Division)
http://www.adamsmith.org.uk/policy/home/htm (Policy Division)
http://www.adamsmith.org.uk/policy/publictions/home.htm (Publications)
http://www.adamsmith.org.uk (Web-Page)

Addenbrooke's NHS Trust (Cambridge)
http://www.addenbrookes.org.uk/ (Web-Page)

Addington, H (Former MP)
http://www.ukpol.co.uk/biooo.htm (Biography)

Adur (Council)
http://www.adurdc.gov.uk/adur.htm (Council Information)
http://www.ukpol.co.uk/adur.htm (Local Election Results (May 1996))
http://www.adurdc.gov.uk/ (Web-Page)

Advisory, Conciliation and Arbitration Service (ACAS)
http://www.coi.gov.uk/coi/depts/GAC/GAC.html (Press Releases)
http://www.coi.gov.uk/coi/depts/GAC/coi9688c.ok (Employment Rights)
http://www.acas.org.uk/ (Web-Page)

Agriculture (Ministry of Agriculture, Fisheries and Food)
http://www.britishmeat.org.uk/ (British Meat On-Line)
http://www.bse.org.uk/ (BSE Information Page)
http://www.maff.gov.uk/aboutmaf/agency/mhs.htm (Meat Hygiene)
http://www.milk.co.uk/ (Milk On-Line)
http://www.maff.gov.uk/aboutmaf/ (Ministerial Information)
http://www.maff.gov.uk/aboutmaf/deprep/cover.htm (Responsibilities)
http://www.maff.gov.uk/aboutmaf/minspech/default.htm (Speeches)
http://www.maff.gov.uk/ (Web-Page)

Aitken, J. [Former MP]
http://www.ukpol.co.uk/biooo.htm (Biography)

Albion Party
http://www.geocities.com/capitolhill/8214/index.htm (Web-Page)

Aldershot (Council)
http://www.ukpol.co.uk/356.htm (Constituency Profile)
http://www.rushmoor.gov.uk/ (Council Web-Page)

Aldridge Brownhills
http://www.ukpol.co.uk/075.htm (Constituency Profile)

Alliance Party
http://www.allianceparty.org/html/faq.html (FAQ)
http://www.allianceparty.org/html/manifesto.html (Manifesto)
http://www.allianceparty.org/html/speeches.html (Speeches)
http://www.allianceparty.org/ (Web-Page)

Alliance For Workers Liberty
http://www.workersliberty.org/otherpub/readings/labour.htm
http://www.workersliberty.org/ (Web-Page)

Alnwick (Council)
http://alnwick.northumberland.gov.uk/ (Web-Page)

Alton, Lord
http://www.ukpol.co.uk/biooo.htm (Biography)

Altrincham & Sale West
http://www.ukpol.co.uk/076.htm (Constituency Profile)

Amber Valley
http://www.ukpol.co.uk/305.htm (Constituency Profile)
http://www.ambervalley.gov.uk/ (Council Web-Page)

Amnesty International
http://www.amnesty.org/ailib/aireport/ar93/index.html (1993 Report)
http://www.amnesty.org/ailib/aireport/ar94/index.html (1994 Report)
http://www.amnesty.org/ailib/aireport/ar95/index.html (1995 Report)
http://www.amnesty.org/ailib/aireport/ar96/index.html (1996 Report)
http://www.amnesty.org/ailib/aireport/ar97/index.html (1997 Report)
http://www.amnesty.org/ailib/aireport/ar98/index.html (1998 Report)
http://www.amnesty.org/ailib/intcam/dp/index.html (Death Penalty1998)
http://www.amnesty.org/ailib/aireport/ar97/eursum.html
(European Section of 1997 Annual Report)
http://www.amnesty.org/campaign/index.html (Current Campaigns)
http://www.amnesty.org/news/index.html (News Releases)
http://www.amnesty.org.uk/ (Web-Page - UK)
http://www.amnesty.org/ (Web-Page - World)

Ancient Monuments Laboratory
http://www.eng-h.gov.uk/ (Web-Page)

Angling
http://www.amnesty.org/ailib/aireport/ar97/eursum.html (Sabotage)
http://envirolink.org/arrs/HSA/features/angling.html (What's wrong with angling HSA)

Angus (Council)
http://www.angus.gov.uk/ (Web-Page)

Anti Fascist Action
http://www.geocities.com/CapitolHill/1884/aaa-links.htm (Web-Site Directory)

Antrim (Council)
http://www.antrim.gov.uk/ (Web-Page)

APCO UK
http://www.apco.co.uk/what/index.htm (About)
http://www.apco.co.uk/menu.htm (List of Ministers and their Shadows)
http://www.apco.co.uk/ (Web-Page)

Argyll & Bute (Council)
http://www.argyll-bute.gov.uk/ (Web-Page)

Armagh (Council)
http://www.armagh.gov.uk/ (Web-Page)

Arts Council

http://www.artscouncil.org.uk/ (Web-Page)

Arun (Council)
http://www.ukpol.co.uk/nlae.htm#A (Previous party make-up)
http://www.arun.gov.uk/ (Web-Page)

Arundel
http://www.ukpol.co.uk/488.htm (Constituency Profile)

Army
http://www.mod.uk/ (Ministry of Defence)
http://www.army.mod.uk/ (Web-Page)

Ashdown, Paddy (Former Leader of the Liberal Democrats)
http://www.ukpol.co.uk/ashdown.htm (Biography)

Ashfield
http://www.ukpol.co.uk/441.htm (Constituency Profile)

Ashford
http://www.ukpol.co.uk/388.htm (Constituency Profile)

Ashton-Under-Lyme
http://www.ukpol.co.uk/77.htm (Constituency Profile)

Assassinations
http://www.ukpol.co.uk/asa.htm (List of Political Assassinations)

Association of University Teachers
http://www.aut.org.uk/dearing2.html (Response to Dearing)
http://www.aut.org.uk/ (Web-Page)

Atomic Energy Authority
http://www.ukaea.org.uk/ (Web-Page)

Audit Commission
http://www.audit-commission.gov.uk/ (Web-Page)

Avon & Somerset Constabulary
http://www.avsom.police.uk/ (Web-Page)

Avon Health Authority
http://www.bristol.digitalcity.org/org/health/ahaweb/ (Web-Page)

Aylesbury
http://www.ukpol.co.uk/274.htm (Constituency Profile)

Baberagh (Council)
http://www.babergh-south-suffolk.gov.uk/bfinance.htm (Finances)
http://www.babergh-south-suffolk.gov.uk/ (Web-Page)

Balfour (Former Prime Minister)
http://www.ukpol.co.uk/balfour.jpg (Picture)

Bank of England

http://www.hm-treasury.gov.uk/pub/html/minutes.html
(Transcript of Monthly Meetings with Chancellor)
http://www.bankofengland.co.uk/ (Web-Page)

Bank of England Bill
http://www.parliament.the-stationery-office.co.uk/pa/ld199798/ldbills/084/1998084.htm

Banking Ombudsman
http://www.obo.org.uk/ (Web-Page)

Barking & Dagenham (Council)
http://www.rmplc.co.uk/eduweb/sites/bandit/index.html (Education)
http://ourworld.compuserve.com/homepages/lbombata/bardag.htm

Barnet (Council)
http://www.barnet.gov.uk/ (Web-Page)

Barnsley (Council)
http://www.shef.ac.uk/~is/barnsley/council/struct.html (Structure)
http://www.shef.ac.uk/~is/barnsley/council/wards.html (Councillors)
http://www.ukpol.co.uk/barnsley.htm (Local Election Results)
http://www.shef.ac.uk/~is/barnsley/council/mps.html (Constituencies)
http://www.ukpol.co.uk/nlae.htm#B (Previous party make-up)
http://www.shef.ac.uk/~is/barnsley/council/council.html (Web-Page)

Basic Income
http://www.vision25.demon.co.uk/pol/bi.htm (Web-Page)

Basingsroke & Deane (Council)
http://www.basingstoke.gov.uk/council/councillors/res120996.htm (1996 local election results)
http://www.basingstoke.gov.uk/council/index.html (Council Information)
http://www.basingstoke.gov.uk/cs/servndx.htm (Index of Local Services)
http://www.ukpol.co.uk/nlae.htm#B (Previous party make-up)
http://www.basingstoke.gov.uk/ (Web-Page)

BBC (See British Broadcasting Corporation)

Bedford (Council)
http://www.bedford.gov.uk/contct01.htm (Council Information)
http://www.bedford.gov.uk/cllrs_01.htm (Councillors)
http://www.bedford.gov.uk/ (Web-Page)

Bedfordshire (Council)
http://www.bedfordshire.gov.uk/ (Web-Page)

Belfast (Council)
http://www.youthservice-belfasteducationandlibraryboard.org.uk/ (Education)
http://www.belfastcity.gov.uk/ (Web-Page)

Benefits Agency
http://www.dss.gov.uk/ba/ (Web-Page)

Berkshire (Council)

http://www.berkshire.gov.uk/ (Web-Page)

Bill of Rights
http://www.open.gov.uk/lcd/speeches/lc4jy97.htm
(Lord Chancellor's speech)

Biotechnology and Biological Sciences Research Council
http://www.bbsrc.ac.uk/ (Web-Page)

Birmingham (Council)
http://www.disability.co.uk/ (Birmingham Disability Resource Centre)
http://birmingham.gov.uk/ (Web-Page)

Blackburn (Council)
http://www.blackburn.gov.uk/ (Web-Page)

Blackpool (Council)
http://www.blackpool.gov.uk/ (Web-Page)

Blair, Tony
http://www.labour.org.uk/information/nec/blair.html (Biography)
http://www.ukpol.co.uk/blair.htm (Biography)
http://www.poptel.org.uk/regeneration/blair.html
(Interview with Regeneration)

Blair Dossier
http://www.geocities.com/~journo/blair.html (Web-Page)

Blood Dossier
http://www.blooddonor.org.uk/ (Web-Page)

Bolsover (Council)
http://dspace.dial.pipex.com/town/parade/taf24 (Web-Page)

Bolton (Council)
http://www.bolton.gov.uk/ (Web-Page)

Book Reviews
http://www.ukpol.co.uk/books.htm (Web-Page)

Bosnia
http://www.fco.gov.uk/bosnia/index.html (British Gvt's position)
http://www.fco.gov.uk/reference/briefs/yugo_chronology.html (Chronology of former Yugoslavia)

Bournemouth (Council)
http://www.bournemouth.gov.uk/ (Web-Page)

Bracknell Forrest (Council)
http://www.bracknell-forest.gov.uk/ (Web-Page)

Bradford (Council)
http://www.bradford.gov.uk/council/ (Council Information)
http://www.bradford.gov.uk/council/the-council/index.htm (Councillors)
http://www.bradford.gov.uk/

Braintree (Council)
http://www.gold.net/users/cs19/

Breckland (Council)
http://www.breckland.gov.uk/

Brent (Council)
http://www.brent.gov.uk/council.htm (About the Council)
http://www.brent.gov.uk/cmte/indxcmte.htm (Council Information)
http://www.brent.gov.uk/

Brentwood (Council)
http://www.brentwood-council.gov.uk/bignews.htm (Borough News)
http://www.brentwood-council.gov.uk/

Brighton (Council)
http://www.brighton-hove.gov.uk/counclrs/wards/welcome.htm
http://www.brighton-hove.gov.uk/welcome.htm

Brighton Health Care NHS Trust
http://www.rscg.org.uk/rsch

Bristol (Council)
http://www.bristol.digitalcity.org/org/council/about-bcc.html
http://www.bristol-city.gov.uk/

Britain out of Europe Campaign
http://www.users.dircon.co.uk/~jonn/britou~1.htm

British Antarctic Survey
http://www.nerc-bas.ac.uk/

British Australian Pensioner Association
http://olis.mtx.net.au/~vicpendis/

British Broadcasting Corporation
http://www.news.bbc.co.uk/ (News Index)
http://www.bbc.co.uk/ (Web-Page)

British Council
http://www.britcoun.org/factfile/index.htm (Fact-File on Britain)
http://www.britcoun.org/uk/uknews.htm (News)
http://www.britcoun.org/scotland (Scotland)
http://www.britcoun.org/wales/welcome.htm (Wales)
http://www.britcoun.org/ (Web-Page)

British Education Communications and Technology Agency
http://www.becta.org.uk/ (Web-Page)

British Left Against Maastricht
http://ourworld.compuserve.com/homepages/redweb/maast.htm

British Library
http://portico.bl.uk/highlights.html (Latest News)

127

http://portico.bl.uk/ (Web-Page)

British Monarchy
http://www.royal.gov.uk/ (Web-Page (Official))

British Museum
http://www.british-museum.ac.uk/ (Web-Page)

British National Party
ftp://ftp.demon.co.uk/pub/doc/liberty/LA/kogbnp.txt (Why we Shouldn't ban the BNP-By Donu Kogbara)
http://www.bnp.to (Midlands Branch)
http://www.bnp.net/ (Web-Page)

British Politics Group
http://www.uc.edu/www/lists/bpg-l/newslet.html (Newsletter)
http://www.uc.edu/www/lists/bpg-l/bpg.html (Web-Page)

British Royal Mint
http://www.royalmint.com/ (Web-Page)

British Standards Institute
http://www.bsi.org.uk/ (Web-Page)

British Tourist Authority
http://www.visitbritain.com/ (Web-Page)

Broadcasting Standards Commission
http://www.bsc.org.uk/ (Web-Page)

Bromsgrove (Council)
http://www.bromsgrove.gov.uk/ (Web-Page)

Broxtowe (Council)
http://www.nottscc.gov.uk/districts/broxtowe/index.htm (Web-Page)

Bruges Group
http://www.eurocritic.demon.co.uk/contents.htm (Web-Page)

BSE Crisis
http://www.bse.org.uk/ (Web-Page)

Buckinghamshire (Council)
http://www.buckscc.gov.uk/ (Web-Page)

Budget
http://www.hm-treasury.gov.uk/pub/html/budget94/speech.html (1994)
http://www.hm-treasury.gov.uk/pub/html/budget.html#1995 (1995)
http://www.hm-treasury.gov.uk/pub/html/budget.html#1996 (1996)
http://www.hm-treasury.gov.uk/pub/html/budget.html (1998)

Building Research Establishment
http://www.bre.co.uk/ (Web-Page)

Burke, Edmund

http://swift.eng.ox.ac.uk/jdr/burke.html (Burke's Page)
http://grid.let.rug.nl/~welling/usa/burke.html (Web-Page)

Burnley (Council)
http://www.burnley.gov.uk/ (Web-Page)

Bury (Council)
http://www.bury.gov.uk/ (Web-Page)

Business for Sterling
http://www.eurocritic.demon.co.uk/bfspress.htm (Web-Page)

Business Link
http://www.businesslink.co.uk/ (Web-Page)

By-Elections
http://www.ukpol.co.uk/byelec.htm (All By-election results)
http://www.ukpol.co.uk/byer.htm (1995 Local by-elections summary)
http://www.ukpol.co.uk/bye.htm (By-election changes since 1979)
http://www.ukpol.co.uk/hem.htm (Hemsworth by-election result)
http://www.ukpol.co.uk/byte.htm (by-election results since August 95)
http://www.ukpol.co.uk/boo1.htm (South East Staffs By-election result)

Cabinet Office
http://www.open.gov.uk/co/cohome.htm (Web-Page)

Cabinet Ministers
http://www.ukpol.co.uk/min.htm (List of Cabinet Ministers since 1900)
http://www.open.gov.uk/m-of-g/minister.htm (Current Cabinet Ministers)

Caerfilly (Council)
http://www.caerphilly.gov.uk/ (Web-Page)

Calderdale (Council)
http://www.calderdale.gov.uk/ (Web-Page)

Callaghan, James (Former Prime Minister)
http://www.ukpol.co.uk/callaghan.htm (Biography)

Cambridge (Council)
http://www.camcnty.gov.uk/sub/az/azindtop.htm (Council Information)
http://www.worldserver.pipex.com/cambridge/ (Web-Page)

Cambridge & Huntingdon Health Authority
http://dialspace.dial.pipex.com/it.chha/ (Web-Page)

Cambridgeshire Council (Council)
http://www.camcnty.gov.uk/ (Web-Page)

Camden (Council)
http://www.camden.gov.uk/ (Web-Page)

Campaign Against Euro Federalism
http://www.poptel.org.uk/against-eurofederalism/ (Web-Page)

Campaign For an Independent Britain
http://web.ukonline.co.uk/stuart.n2/campaign/ (Campaign [Journal])
http://www.keele.ac.uk/socs/ks40/cibnw.htm (North West Branch)
http://www.almac.co.uk/diversity/scotcib/scotcib.html (Scottish Branch)
http://www.netenterprises.co.uk/cib/ (South-East Branch)
http://www.bullen.demon.co.uk/index.htm (Web-Page)

Campaign for Political Ecology
http://www.gn.apc.org/eco/eview/eview.html (Newsletter)
http://www.gn.apc.org/eco/ (Web-Page)

Campaign For Seperation of Church and State
http://www.angelfire.com/pa/churchandstate/ (Web-Page)

Capital Punishment
http://www.abolition-now.com/ (Anti Capital-Punishment Article)
http://maristb.marist.edu/~en110/@httpd/cappun.html
(Pro Capital-Punishment Article)
http://www.yahoo.com/Society_and_Culture/Crime/Death_Penalty/ (Yahoo list of links)

Caradon (Council)
http://www.caradon.gov.uk/ (Web-Page)

Cardiff (Council)
http://www.cardiff.gov.uk/ (Web-Page)

Carlisle (Council)
http://www.carlisle-city.gov.uk/ (Web-Page)

Carlton Publishing
http://www.carlton-group.co.uk/ (Web-Page)

Carmarthanshire (Council)
http://www.carmarthenshire.gov.uk/ (Web-Page)

CARRICKFERGUS: (Council)
http://www.carrickfergus.org/ (Web-Page)

Castle Morpeth (Council)
http://www.castlemorpeth.gov.uk/ (Web-Page)

Castlereagh (Council)
http://www.castlereagh.gov.uk/ (Web-Page)

CCTA (Central Computing and Telecommunications Agency)
http://www.ccta.gov.uk/ (Web-Page)

Celtic League
http://www.manxman.co.im/cleague (Web-Page)

Census Information Gateway
http://census.ac.uk/ (Web-Page)

Central Adjudication Service
http://www.cas.gov.uk/ (Web-Page)

Central Office of Information
http://www.coi.gov.uk/coi/depts/deptlist.html (Press Releases)
http://www.coi.gov.uk/coi/ (Web-Page)

Central Science Laboratory
http://www.csl.gov.uk/ (Web-Page)

Centre For Citizenship
http://home.clara.net/citizen/family.html (Condemnation of Monarchy)
http://home.clara.net/citizen/news.html (News)
http://home.clara.net/citizen/ (Web-Page)

Centre For Reform
http://www.cfr.org.uk/publications.html (Publications)
http://www.cfr.org.uk/ (Web-Page)

Ceredigion (Council)
http://www.ceredigion.gov.uk/ (Web-Page)

Chancellor of the Exchequer
http://www.hm-treasury.gov.uk/pub/html/profiles/chexbio.html (Biog)
http://www.hm-treasury.gov.uk/pub/html/speech/chex.html (Speeches)
http://www.hm-treasury.gov.uk/pub/html/chxstatmt/main.html
http://www.hm-treasury.gov.uk/ (Treasury Web-Page)

Chard (Council)
http://www.chard.gov.uk/introduction.html (Web-Page)

Charity Commission
http://www.charity-commission.gov.uk/ccabout.htm
http://www.charity-commission.gov.uk/characts.htm (Charities Act)
http://www.charity-commission.gov.uk/ (Web-Page)

Charnwood (Council)
http://www.charnwoodbc.gov.uk/ (Web-Page)

Charter 88
http://www.gn.apc.org/charter88/press/whatsnew.html (News)
http://www.gn.apc.org/charter88/press/press.html (Press Releases)
http://www.gn.apc.org/charter88/index.html (Web-Page)

Chelmsford (Council)
http://www.chelmsfordbc.gov.uk/ (Web-Page)
http://www.chelmsfordbc.gov.uk/council/council.htm (Committees)

Cheltenham (Council)
http://www.cheltenham.gov.uk/ (Web-Page)

Cherwell (Council)
http://www.cherwell-dc.gov.uk/ (Web-Page)

Cheshire (Council)
http://www.u-net.com/cheshire/county/council.htm
http://www.u-net.com/cheshire/ (Web-Page)

Chester (Council)
http://www.chestercc.gov.uk/ (Web-Page)

Chesterfield (Council)
http:/www.chesterfieldbc.gov.uk/ (Web-Page)

Chichester (Council)
http://www.chicester.gov.uk/ (Web-Page)

Child Support Agency
http://www.dss.gov.uk/csa/cschart.htm (Citizen's Charter)
http://www.dss.gov.uk/csa/index.htm (Web-Page)

Chipping Camden (Council)
http://www.chippingcampden.co.uk/ (Web-Page)

Christchurch (Council)
http://www.dorset-cc.gov.uk/xchurcl.htm (Web-Page)

Christian Heritage Party
http://ourworld.compuserve.com/homepages/avant/content.htm

Christianity and Politics
http://www.users.dircon.co.uk/~ajbb/ (Web-Page)

Church of England
http://www.church-of-england.org/ (Web-Page)

Churchill, Winston
http://www.grolier.com/wwii/wwii_churchill.html (Biography)
http://www.churchill-society-london.org.uk/index.html (Churchill Society)
http://www.empirenet.com/~rdaeley/authors/churchill.html (Web-Page)

Citizen's Charters
http://www.open.gov.uk/charter/winners.htm (Charter Mark 1995)
http://www.open.gov.uk/charter/list.htm (Index of Charters)
http://www.servicefirst.gov.uk/ (Web-Page)

CND
http://www.abdn.ac.uk/~src022/news.html (News)
http://www.abdn.ac.uk/~src022/ (Web-Page)

Coal Authority
http://www.coal.gov.uk/ (Web-Page)

Coastguard Agency
http://www.coastguard.gov.uk/ (Web-Page)

Colchester (Council)
http://www.colchester.gov.uk/ (Web-Page)

Commission For New Towns
http://www.cnt.org.uk/ (Web-Page)

Commission For Racial Equality

http://www.open.gov.uk/cre/whatis2.htm (About)
http://www.open.gov.uk/cre/crehome.htm (Web-Page)

Commons (See under House of Commons)

Commonwealth Foundation
http://www.oneworld.org/com_fnd/ (Web-Page)

Commonwealth Institute
http://www.commonwealth.org.uk/ (Web-Page)

Commonwealth On-line
http://www.tcol.co.uk/ (Web-Page)

Commonwealth War Graves Commission
http://www.cwgc.org/ (Web-Page)

Communist Party
http://ourworld.compuserve.com/homepages/redweb/

Communist Party of Great Britain
http://members.xoom.com/cpgb/ (Sheffield Branch)
http://www.totalweb.co.uk/cp-of-britain/index.html (Web-Page)
http://www.duntone.demon.co.uk/CPGB/index.html (Web-Page)

Companies House
http://www.companies-house.gov.uk/ (Web-Page)

Conservative Parliamentarians
http://www.shef.ac.uk/uni/academic/N-Q/pol/EUROTORY.HTML (Web-Page)

Conservative Party
http://www.conservative-party.org.uk/ (Web-Page)
http://www.ukpol.co.uk/cpl.htm (Leaders of the Conservative Party)
http://www.ukpol.co.uk/rop.htm (About the Conservative Party)
http://www.ivytech.co.uk/torywin/ (Tory Win 2002)
http://ourworld.compuserve.com/homepages/Paul_Watkins/ (Barnsley West Association)
http://www.netlink.co.uk/users/horgan/bascon/ (Basildon Conservative Association)
http://www.conservative-party.org.uk/partyorg/nhsnet/ (The Conservative NHS Network)
http://www.city.ac.uk/~ep187/city.html (City University Conservative Association)
http://www.the2000foundation.org.uk/ (Conservative 2000 Foundation)
http://homepages.enterprise.net/prospero/conwy.html (Conwy Conservative Association)
http://www.conwayfor.org/ (Conservative Way Forward)
http://ourworld.compuserve.com/homepages/Darlington_Conservative_Assn/ (Darlington)
http://www.mic.dundee.ac.uk/dusa/soc9.html (Dundee University Conservatives)
http://www.city.ac.uk/~ep187/esyc.html (Enfield-Southgate Young Conservatives)
http://www.atlas.co.uk/enfieldyc/ (Enfield North Young Conservatives)
http://master.www.cityscape.co.uk:1081/users/fd15/index.html (Epping Forest Young)
http://www.conservative-party.org.uk/Constituency_Pages/finchley_gold/ (Finchley)
http://www.conservative-party.org.uk/Constituency_Pages/gosport/index.html (Gosport)
http://www.city.ac.uk/~dn514/gla_cs.html (Greater London Area Conservative Students)
http://ourworld.compuserve.com/homepages/glyc/ (Greater London Young Conservatives)
http://www.nwh-tories.org.uk/ (North West Hampshire Conservative Association)

http://www.slco.demon.co.uk/conass.htm (Havant Conservative Association)
http://www.conservative-party.org.uk/history/hist_01.htm (History)
http://www.keele.ac.uk/socs/ks20/home.htm (Keele University Conservative Association)
http://alethea.ukc.ac.uk/SU/Societies/KUCA/ (Kent University Conservative Association)
http://www.conservative-party.org.uk/Constituency_Pages/lambeth/index.html (Lambeth)
http://www.ukpol.co.uk/jmwa.htm (List of Conservative Associations)
http://www.conservative-party.org.uk/westmstr/meps.htm (List of Conservative MEPs)
http://www.conservative-party.org.uk/mpsname/mpsname.htm (List of Conservative MPs)
http://www.mikhutch.demon.co.uk/mcacb.htm (Maidenhead Conservative Association)
http://www.ukpol.co.uk/conf.htm (Membership of the Conservative Party
http://member.aol.com/nefca/index.html (North East Fife Conservative Association)
http://www.conservative-party.org.uk/Constituency_Pages/Norwich_North/index.html
(Norwich North)
http://www.conservative-party.org.uk/Constituency_Pages/Oxford_East/index.html
(Oxford East
http://www.conservative-party.org.uk/Constituency_Pages/Oxford_West/index.html
(Oxford est)
http://www.conservative-party.org.uk/Constituency_Pages/Skipton_Ripon/index.html
(Skipton Conservatives)
http://www.st-and.ac.uk/~www_sa/socs/stauca/tory.html (St. Andrew's University)
http://www.conservative-party.org.uk/Constituency_Pages/southampton/index.html
(Southampton
http://www.ukpol.co.uk/jmwa.htm (Student Conservative Associations)
http://www.ukpol.co.uk/boo2.htm (Tory candidates standing at the 1997 General Election)
http://www.csv.warwick.ac.uk/~suaba/ (Warwick University Conservative Association
http://www.conservative-party.org.uk/ (Web-Page)
http://www.conservative-party.org.uk/Constituency_Pages/wells/index.html (Wells)
http://ourworld.compuserve.com/homepages/Welwyn_Hatfield_Conservatives/
(Welwyn Hatfield)
http://www.conservative-party.org.uk/Constituency_Pages/west_lancashire/index.html
(West Lancashire)
http://www.york.ac.uk/~socs35/ (York University Conservative Association)

Conservative Way Forward
http://www.conwayfor.org/forward.html (Forward (Magazine
http://www.conwayfor.org/ (Web-Page)

Conservatives Against a Federal Europe
http://www.cafe.org.uk/ (Web-Page)

Constitutional Documents
http://portico.bl.uk/access/treasures/magna-carta.html (Magna Carta)

Contaminated Ground
http://www.contaminatedland.co.uk/ (Web-Page)

Contributions Agency
http://www.dss.gov.uk/ca (Web-Page)

Convention of Scottish Local Authorities
http://www.cosla.gov.uk/ (Web-Page)

Cook, Robin
http://www.ukpol.co.uk/cook.htm (Biography)

Cornwall (Council)
http://www.cornwall.gov.uk/ (Web-Page)

Council Tax
http://www.open.gov.uk/doe/lgfp/flas/keystats.htm#bands (Council Tax Bands)
http://www.open.gov.uk/doe/lgfp/flas/keystats.htm#cap (Council Tax Capping)
http://www.open.gov.uk/doe/lgfp/flas/keystats.htm#ctc (Council Tax Collection)
http://www.open.gov.uk/doe/lgfp/flt/ctax967.htm (Council Tax Charges for 1996/7)
http://www.local.doe.gov.uk/finance/ctax/ctax.htm (Government Guide)

Countryside Commission
http://www.countryside.gov.uk/ (Web-Page)

Countryside Council For Wales
http://www.ccw.gov.uk/ (Web-Page)

Court Service
http://www.open.gov.uk/courts/charter/courts.htm (Citizen's Charters for the Courts)
http://www.open.gov.uk/courts/court/cs_home.htm (Web-Page)

Coventry (Council)
http://www.coventry.gov.uk/intro/intro.html (Council Information)
http://www.coventry.gov.uk/ (Web-Page)

Craigavon (Council)
http://www.craigavon.gov.uk/ (Web-Page)

Crewe and Nantwich (Council)
http://www.ukpol.co.uk/crewe.htm (1996 Local Election Results)
http://www.ukpol.co.uk/nlae.htm#C (Previous Party make-up for Crewe and Nantwich)
http://www.netcentral.co.uk/~cnbc/ (Web-Page))

Crime Statistics
http://www.ukpol.co.uk/crime.htm (Crime (Recorded) figures since 1951)
http://www.open.gov.uk/home_off/rsdhome.htm (Home Office Statistics)

Crimestoppers
http://www.worldserver.pipex.com/crimestoppers/ (Web-Page)

Criminal Justice System
http://www.open.gov.uk/home_off/rsdhome.htm (Home Office Research and Statistics)
http://envirolink.org/arrs/HSA/news/cjaleic.html (Hunt Saboteurs Association condemn)
http://www.ukpol.co.uk/pri.htm (Prison Populations, 1900-1990)
http://www.ukpol.co.uk/crime.htm (Recorded crimes 1950-1994)

Critical European Group
http://www.keele.ac.uk/socs/ks40/ceghome.html (Web-Page)

Crown Prosecution Service
http://www.cps.gov.uk/ (Web-Page)

Croydon (Council)
http://clip.croydon.gov.uk/index-living.htm (Education)
http://clip.croydon.gov.uk/cr-counc.htm (Web-Page)

Cullen Report
http://www.the-stationery-office.co.uk/document/scottish/dunblane/dunblane.htm

Culture, Media and Sport
http://www.culture.gov.uk/corpinfo.htm (Responsibilities of Department)
http://www.culture.gov.uk/ (Web-Page)

Cumbria (Council)
http://www.cumbria.gov.uk/ (Web-Page)

Cumbria Tourist Board
http://www.cumbria-tourist-board.org.uk/ctb (Web-Page)

Cunningham, Jack (Agriculture Secretary)
http://www.ukpol.co.uk/cun.htm (Biography)

Customs & Excise
http://www.coi.gov.uk/coi/depts/GCE/GCE.html (Press Releases)
http://www.hmce.gov.uk/

Cymidenthas Yr Iath Cymreag
http://www.aber.uk/~iis5/taford.html (Web-Page)

Cymru Goch
http://www.fanergoch.org (Web-Page)

Daresbury
http://www.dl.ac.uk/ (Web-Page)

Darlington (Council)
http://www.darlington.org.uk/council/ (Web-Page)

Data Protection Registrar
http://www.open.gov.uk/dpr/dprhome.htm (Web-Page)

David Boothroyd's Politics and Elections Page
http://www.election.demon.co.uk/ (Web-Page)

Defence, Ministry of
http://www.mod.uk/def_wp95/def_wp95.htm (1995 White Paper)
http://www.mod.uk/def_wp96/def_wp96.htm (1996 White Paper)
http://www.mod.uk/archive/archive.htm (Archive)
http://www.army.mod.uk/ (British Army)
http://www.mod.uk/commercial/commercial.htm (Commercial Tendering Process)
http://www.mod.uk/policy/gulfwar/index.htm (Gulf War Veterans)
http://www.mod.uk/sofs.htm (Ministers)
http://www.mod.uk/speeches/speech.htm (Policies)
http://www.mod.uk/aboutmod/ (Press Releases)
http://www.raf.mod.uk/ (Royal Air Force)
http://www.royal-navy.mod.uk/ (Royal Navy)

http://www.mod.uk/other.htm (Speeches)
http://www.mod.uk/policy/sdr/index.htm (Strategic Defence Review)
http://www.mod.uk/ (Web-Page)

Democratic Left
http://www.gn.apc.org/demleft/ (Web-Page)

Demos
http://www.demos.co.uk/ (Web-Page)

Denbighshire (Council)
http://www.denbighshire.gov.uk/ (Web-Page)

Department For Education And Employment
http://www.hmis.scotoff.gov.uk/ (Education in Scotland)
http://www.wales.gov.uk/groupframe.html (Education in Wales)
http://www.employmentservice.gov.uk (Employment Service)
http://www.lowpay.gov.uk (Low Pay Commission)
http://www.dfee.gov.uk/miniresp.htm (Ministerial Information)
http://www.newdeal.gov.uk/ (New Deal)
http://www.dfee.gov.uk/news/press.htm (Press Releases)
http://www.dfee.gov.uk/news/53.htm (Spending Plans)
http://www.teach.org.uk/ (teach.org)
http://www.teach-tta.gov.uk/ (Teacher Training Agency)
http://www.dfee.gov.uk/ (Web-Page)

Department of the Environment Transport and the Regions
http://www.environment.detr.gov.uk/epsim/index.htm (Environment in Facts and Figures)
http://www.local-transport.detr.gov.uk/ (Local Transport)
http://www.detr.gov.uk/thisis/4.htm (Ministerial Information)
http://www.nds.coi.gov.uk/coi/coipress.htm (Press Releases)
http://www.detr.gov.uk/thisis/detr.htm (Responsibilities of Department)
http://www.detr.gov.uk/pubs/index.htm (Speeches)
http://www.dwi.detr.gov.uk/h2oinfo.htm (Water Industry Information)
http://www.detr.gov.uk/ (Web-Page)

Department of Health
http://www.open.gov.uk/doh/hon..htm (Health of the Nation)
http://www.ukpol.co.uk/min.htm#hss (List of Health Cabinet Ministers this century)
http://www.doh.gov.uk/minister/minister.htm (Ministerial Information)
http://www.nhs50/nhs.uk/ (NHS 50)
http://www.coi.gov.uk/coi/depts/GDH/GDH.html (Press Releases)
http://www.doh.gov.uk/about.htm (Responsibilities of Department)
http://www.doh.gov.uk/ (Web-Page)

Department of international Development
http://www.dfid.gov.uk/ (Web-Page)

Department of Social Security
http://www.dss.gov.uk/ (Web-Page)

Department of Trade and Industry

http://www.dti.gov.uk/Ministers.html (Ministers)
http://www.coi.gov.uk/coi/depts/GTI/GTI.html (Press Releases)
http://www.dti.gov.uk/Publications.html (Publications on the Internet)
http://www.dti.gov.uk/Speeches.html (Speeches)
http://www.dti.gov.uk/ (Web-Page)

Deputy Prime Minister
http://www.ukpol.co.uk/min.htm#Deputy (List of Deputy Prime Ministers this century)

Deregulation Initiative
http://www.open.gov.uk/co/du/duhome.htm (Web-Page)

Derwentshire (Council)
http://www.derwentshire.org.uk/ (Web-Page)

Deselected MPs
http://www.ukpol.co.uk/den.htm (MPs denied renomination in 1997 by their political party)

Design Council
http://www.design-council.org.uk/ (Web-Page)

Devolution
http://www.record-mail.co.uk/rm/devo/ (Daily Record)

Devon (Council)
http://www.devon-cc.gov.uk/dris/home-page.html (General Information)
http://www.devon-cc.gov.uk/ (Web-Page)

Diana, Princess of Wales
http://www.althorp-house.co.uk/ (Althorp House)
http://www.bbc.co.uk/ (BBC News Diana Archive)
http://www.dianagarden.org.uk/ (Kensington Garden Consultation)
http://www.royal.gov.uk/start.htm (Monarchy Web-Page)

DIsraeli, Benjamin
http://www.usc.edu/dept/history/huffman/disraeli/disraeli/life.htm (Biography)

Dissolution Honours 1997
http://www.ukpol.co.uk/hon..htm (List of Honours)

Donations to Political Parties
http://users.powernet.co.uk/hack/sleaze/ (List of Companies Donating Money)

Dorset (Council)
http://www.dorset-cc.gov.uk/works.htm (Council Information)
http://www.dorset-cc.gov.uk / (Web-Page)

Dorset Health Authority
http://www.dorset.swest.nhs.uk/ (Web-Page)

Downing Street
http://www.number-10.gov.uk/ (10 Downing Street Web-Page)
http://www.open.gov.uk/co/cohome.htm (Cabinet Office)

Downing Street Declaration
http://www.bess.tcd.ie/dclrtn.htm (Text)

Driving and Vehicle Licensing Agency
http://www.open.gov.uk/dvla/index.htm (Web-Page)

Dudley (Council)
http://www.edu.dudley.gov.uk/ (Education)
http://www.dudley.gov.uk/ (Web-Page)

Dumfries & Galloway (Council)
http://www.dumgal.gov.uk/ (Web-Page)

Dundee (Council)
http://www.dundeecity.gov.uk/ (Web-Page)

Dungannon (Council)
http://www.dungannon.gov.uk/ (Web-Page)

Durham (Council)
http://www.durhamcity.gov.uk/ (Web-Page Durham City Council)
http://www.durham.gov.uk (Web-Page Durham County Council)

Durham Constabulary
http://www.durham.police.uk/ (Web-Page)

DVLA:
http://www.open.gov.uk/dvla/index.htm (Web-Page)

Dyfed-Powys (Council)
http://www.dyfed-powys.police.uk/ (Web-Page)

Ealing (Council)
http://www.ealing.gov.uk/ (Web-Page)

East Devon (Council)
http://www.east-devon.gov.uk/ (Web-Page)

East Dorset (Council)
http://www.eastdorsetdc.gov.uk/ (Web-Page)

East Dunbartonshire (Council)
http://ourworld.compuserve.com/homepages/strathkelvin/welcome.htm (Web-Page)

East Grinstead Town Council (Council)
http://www.egnet.co.uk/egtc/ (Web-Page)

East Hampshire (Council)
http://www.townpages.org/ehdc/counclrs.htm (List of Councillors)
http://www.townpages.org/ehdc/index.htm (Web-Page)

East Midlands Network
http://www.emnet.co.uk/ (Web-Page)

East Northamptonshire (Council)

http://www.east-northamptonshire.gov.uk/ (Web-Page)

East Renfrewshire (Council)
http://www.eastrenfrewshire.gov.uk/ (Web-Page)

East Riding of Yorkshire (Council)
http://www.east-riding-of-yorkshire.gov.uk/ (Web-Page)

East Sussex (Council)
http://www.eastsussexcc.gov.uk/ (Web-Page)

Easington (Council)
http://www.easington.gov.uk/ (Web-Page)

Eastern Surrey Health Commission
http://www.surreycc.gov.uk/eshc/ (Web-Page)

Ecology and Hydrology Centre
http://www.nmw.ac.uk/ceh/ (Web-Page)

Economic and Social Research Council
http://sosig.ac.uk/Esrc/esrc.html (Web-Page)

Economy
http://www.hm-treasury.gov.uk/pub/html/budget94/speech.html (1994 Budget)
http://www.hm-treasury.gov.uk/pub/html/budget.html (1995 Budget)
http://www.hm-treasury.gov.uk/pub/html/debt/main.html (Debt Management Reports)
http://www.hm-treasury.gov.uk/pub/html/econbf/main.html (Treasury Economic Briefings)

Eden (Council)
http://www.eden.gov.uk/eden-dc/ (Web-Page)

Edinburgh (Council)
http://www.efr.hw.ac.uk/EDC/Edinburgh.html (Web-Page)

Education
http://www.open.gov.uk/dfee/dfeehome.htm (Department of Education and Employment)
http://www.ed.ac.uk/~riu/GETS/index.html (Education and Training in Scotland)
http://www.coi.gov.uk/coi/depts/GDE/coi2736c.ok (Information about Work-Fare)
http://www.ukpol.co.uk/min.htm#edu (List of Education Cabinet Ministers this century)

Education On-Line
http://www.leeds.ac.uk/educol/ (Web-Page)

Elections
http://www.ukpol.co.uk/nbfj.htm#gen (General)
http://www.ukpol.co.uk/nbks.htm#local (Local)
http://www.ukpol.co.uk/nbae.htm#by (By-Elections)
http://www.ukpol.co.uk/nbks.htm#ni (Northern Ireland)
http://www.ukpol.co.uk/nbae.htm#eur (European Elections)

Electoral Reform Society
http://www.gn.apc.org/ers/ (Web-Page)

Electoral Systems

http://www.psr.keele.ac.uk/ (Richard Kimber's Web-Page)

Embassy
http://britain.nyc.ny.us/ (British Embassy in the U.S.)

Employment
http://www.open.gov.uk/dfee/dfeehome.htm (Department of Employment and Education)
http://www.ukpol.co.uk/min.htm#edue (List of Education and Employment Ministers this century)

Employment Service
http://www.laser.employmentservice.gov.uk/ (London and South East)
http://www.northern.employmentservice.gov.uk/ (Northern Region)
http://www.employmentservice.gov.uk/ (Web-Page)

EMU (European Monetary Union)
http://www.abelard.org/emu/emu-hi.htm (Why EMU is bad)

Enfield (Council)
http://www.enfield.gov.uk/ (Web-Page)

Engineering Council
http://www.engc.org.uk/ (Web-Page)

English Heritage
http://www.english-heritage.org.uk/ (Web-Page)

English Nature
http://www.english-nature.org.uk/ (Web-Page)

English Sports Council
http://www.english.sports.gov.uk/ (Web-Page)

Enterprise Zone
http://www.enterprisezone.org.uk/ (Web-Page)

Envirolink
http://www.envirolink.org/ (Web-Page)

Environment, Department of
http://www.detr.gov.uk/ (Web-Page)

Environment Agency
http://www.environment-agency.gov.uk/ (Web-Page)

Epson & Ewell (Council)
http://www.surreyweb.org.uk/epsombc/members.htm (Councillors)
http://www.surreyweb.org.uk/epsombc/ (Web-Page)

Equal Opportunities Commission
http://www.eoc.org.uk/ (Web-Page)

Essex (Council)
http://www.essexcc.gov.uk/ (Web-Page)

Euro
http://www.euro.gov.uk/ (Official UK Government Site)

Europe
http://www.fco.gov.uk/europe/Britain in the EU (Foreign Office)
http://www.ukpol.co.uk/cec.htm (British Contributions to the EEC/EC/EU)
http://www.ukpol.co.uk/chr.htm (Chronology of Events in the EEC/EC/EU from 1948 to 1996)
http://adhocalypse.arts.unimelb.edu.au/fcf/ucr/student/1996/j.greenall/ (EU and Britain-A study)
http://europa.eu.int/welcome.html (E.U.Web-Page)
http://www.math.uio.no/faq/european-union/basics/part1.htm (FAQ: in eight parts.)
http://www.ukpol.co.uk/ref.htm (Referendum Result)
http://www.conwayfor.org/FORWARD/01_1991/shackles.html (Shackles of E.M.U. (Patrick Minford))
http://www.apco.co.uk/whoswho/index.htm (Who's Who in the E.U. (A.P.C.O.))

European Convention For the Protection of Pet Animals
http://www.cdb.org/euro.htm (Web-Page)

European Elections
http://www.election.demon.co.uk/ep1994.html (1994 European Election Results for the UK)
http://www.unite.net/customers/alliance/elfull.html (N.Ireland results since 1979)

European Environmental Agency
http://www.eea.dk/default.htm (Web-Page)

European Monetary Union
http://www.abelard.org/emu/emu-hi.htm (Why EMU is bad)

European Parliament
http://www.europarl.eu.int/ (Web-Page)

European Union
http://www.europarl.eu.int/dg7/igc/en/pos-toc.htm (Summary of Member States views on the IGC)

European Union Follies and Myths
http://www.kc3ltd.co.uk/profile/eurofollie/ (Web-Page)

Evangelica Christianity and British Politics
http://www.users.dircon.co.uk/~ajbb/ (Web-Page)

Export Credits Gurentee Department
http://www.open.gov.uk/ecgd/index.htm (Web-Page)

Fabian Society
http://users.ox.ac.uk/~kebl0613/fab1.html (Oxford University Branch)
http://www.fabian-society.org.uk/ (Web-Page)

Fabricant Michael (MP for Lichfield)
http://www.solnet.co.uk/fabricant (Web-Page)

Falkirk (Council)
http://www.heartofscotland.org.uk/fve/services/providers/falkirk_ds.html (Web-Page)

Fareham (Council)
http://ourworld.compuserve.com/homepages/fareham_borough_council/thecounc.htm
(Council Information)
http://ourworld.compuserve.com/homepages/farehambc2/BMAP.htm (Councillors)
http://ourworld.compuserve.com/homepages/farehambc2/BMAYOR.htm (Mayor)
http://ourworld.compuserve.com/homepages/farehambc2/BGROUP.htm (Party Make-Up on Council)
http://ourworld.compuserve.com/homepages/fareham_borough_council/ (Web-Page)

Farnborough (Council)
http://www.rushmoor.gov.uk/ (Web-Page Farnborough, Rushmoor)

Fascism (History):
http://www.merepseud.mcmail.com/ (Web-Page)

Federation of Small Businesses
http://www.fsb.org.uk/introduction.htm (Web-Page)

Felixstowe (Council)
http://www.felixstowe.gov.uk/ (Web-Page)

Fermanagh (Council)
http://www.fermanagh.gov.uk/ (Web-Page)

Field, Frank (Former Social Security Minister)
http://www.dss.gov.uk/hq/ffield.htm (Biography)
http://www.unemployment.co.uk/ (Right-to-Work)
http://www.dss.gov.uk/ (Social Security Web-Page)

Financial Services Authority
http://www.fsa.gov.uk/ (Web-Page)

Flintshire (Council)
http://www.flintshire.gov.uk/ (Web-Page)

Follett, barbara MP
http://www.poptel.org.uk/barbara.follett/ (Web-Page)

Foreign and Commonwealth Office
http://www.fco.gov.uk/ (Web-Page)
http://www.fco.gov.uk/aboutfco/ (About the Foreign Office)
http://www.fco.gov.uk/bosnia/index.html (Bosnia and Britain)
http://www.fco.gov.uk/france-gb/index.html (France and Britain)
http://www.fco.gov.uk/current/1997/feb/10/latinam.txt (Latin America and Britain)
http://www.fco.gov.uk/un/index.html (United Nations and Britain)
http://www.fco.gov.uk/weu/index.html (Western European Union and Britain)
http://www.fco.gov.uk/current/thismonth.html (What's New)

Foresight
http://www.foresight.gov.uk/ (Web-Page)

Forest of Dean (Council)
http://www.demon.co.uk/fweb/fddc/ (Web-Page)

Forestry Commission
http://www.forestry.gov.uk/ (Web-Page)

Forward Magazine
http://www.conway.for.org/information.html (Web-Page)

Free Britain
http://www.freebrit.demon.co.uk (Web-Page)

Freedom Association
http://www.pipemedia.net/~freedom/tp/ftoday.htm (*Freedom* Today [Journal])
http://www.pipemedia.net/~freedom/FREEDOM.htm (Web-Page)

Freedom of Information Unit
http://www.open.gov.uk/m-of-g/foihome.htm (Web-Page)

Friends of the Earth
http://www.foe.co.uk/nirexrcf/index.html (FotE and Nirex)
http://www.foe.co.uk/action/newbury/index.html (Newbury By-Pass)
http://www.foe.co.uk/pubsinfo/infosyst/index.html (Policies)
http://www.foe.co.uk/pubsinfo/infoteam/pressrel/index.html (Press Releases)
http://www.foe.co.uk/ (Web-Page)

Fundamentally Green
http://www.barnsdle.demon.co.uk/pol/fundi.html (Web-Page)

Further Education and Funding Council
http://www.fefc.ac.uk/ (Web-Page)

Gallup
http://www.gallup.com/ (Web-Page)

Gateshead (Council)
http://www.gatesheadmbc.gov.uk/ (Web-Page)

General Elections
http://www.qmw.ac.uk/~laws/election/allbritmp.html (List of M.P.s)
http://www.ukpol.co.uk/los.htm (Lowest number of votes in a Parliamentary Election)
http://www.unite.net/customers/alliance/elfull.html#wmst (N. Ireland results)
http://www.warwick.ac.uk/~esrhi/vote/ukRes.html (Results since 1945)
http://www.qmw.ac.uk/~laws/election/index.html (Results since 1983)
http://www.ukpol.co.uk/gen.htm#1945 (1945)
http://www.ukpol.co.uk/gen.htm#1950 (1950)
http://www.ukpol.co.uk/gen.htm#1951 (1951)
http://www.ukpol.co.uk/gen.htm#1955 (1955)
http://www.keele.ac.uk/depts/po/ge97.htm (1997 Election archive)

Glan Clywd District General Hospital NHS Trust
http://www.glanclwyd.demon.co.uk/ (Web-Page)

Glasgow (Council)

http://www.glasgow.gov.uk/ (Web-Page)

Gloucestershire (Council)
http://www.gloscc.gov.uk/gcc.htm (Council Information)
http://www.gloscc.gov.uk/cteeserv/index.htm (Councillors)
http://www.gloscc.gov.uk/election/index.htm (Election News)
http://www.gloscc.gov.uk/ (Web-Page)

Gosport (Council)
http://www.gosport.gov.uk/ (Web-Page)

Government Communications Headquarters
http://www.gchq.gov.uk/ (Web-Page)

Government Information Server
http://www.open.gov.uk/ (Web-Page)

Government Office For the West Midlands
http://www.go-wm.gov.uk/ (Web-Page)

Graphicl Paper and Media Union
http://www.gpmu.org.uk/campaign.html (Campaigns)
http://www.gpmu.org.uk/ (Web-Page)

Greater Manchester Police
http://www.gmp.police.uk/ (Web-Page)

Green Net
http://www.gn.apc.org/ (Web-Page)

Green Party
http://www.gn.apc.org/greenparty/policy/mfss/ (Manifesto)
http://www.gn.apc.org/greenparty/ (Web-Page)
http://www.greenparty.org.uk/ (Web-Page)

Geenpeace
http://www.greenpeace.org/ (Web-Page)

Greenwich (Council)
http://www.greenwich.gov.uk/ (Web-Page)

Grooundwork
http://www.groundwork.org.uk/press.html (Latest News)
http://www.groundwork.org.uk/ (Web-Page)

Guildford (Council)
http://www.surreyweb.org.uk/guildfordbc/guild1.html (Council Information)
http://www.surreyweb.org.uk/guildfordbc/ (Web-Page)

Gwynedd (Council)
http://www.gwynedd.gov.uk/index.english.html (Web-Page)

Hackney (Council)
http://www.hackney.gov.uk/wards/Wards.html (Council Information)
http://www.hackney.gov.uk/ (Web-Page)

Hague, William
http://www.ukpol.co.uk/hague.htm (Biography)
http://www.ukpol.co.uk/hag.htm (Hague to play important role in 1997 election)

Hamilton, Neil
http://www.ukpol.co.uk/hama.htm (Article by Nigel Fletcher)
http://www.neilhamilton.co.uk/ (Official Web-Site)

Hammersmith and Fulham (Council)
http://www.lbhf.gov.uk/ (Web-Page)

Hampshire (Council)
http://www.hants.gov.uk/business.html (Business in Hampshire)
http://www.hants.gov.uk/localgov/cllrs.html (Councillors and Minutes)
http://www.hants.gov.uk/educate.html (Education in Hampshire)
http://www.hants.gov.uk/health.html (Health in Hampshire)
http://www.hants.gov.uk/localgov.html (Local Gvt in Hampshire)
http://www.hants.gov.uk/socserv.html (Social Services in Hampshire)
http://www.hants.gov.uk/ (Web-Page)

Hansard (House of Commons)
http://www.parliament.the-stationery-office.co.uk/pa/cm/cmhansrd.htm (Web-Page)

Hansard (House of Lords)
http://www.parliament.the-stationery-office.co.uk/pa/ld/ldhansrd.htm (Web-Page)

Haringey (Council)
http://www.haringey.gov.uk/ (Web-Page)

Harlow (Council)
http://www.harlow.gov.uk/hdc/introhdc.htm (Council Information)
http://www.harlow.gov.uk/hdc/cllrs.htm (Councillors)
http://www.harlow.gov.uk/ (Web-Page)

Harman, Harriet (Former Social Security Secretary)
http://www.ukpol.co.uk/harman.htm (Biography)

Harrow (Council)
http://www.harrowlb.demon.co.uk/ (Web-Page)

Hart (Council)
http://www.c2000.com/hartdc/minutes.htm (Council and Committee Minutes)
http://www.c2000.com/hartdc/index.htm (Web-Page)

Hatings (Council)
http://www.hastings.gov.uk/ (Web-Page)

Hastings and Rother NHS Trust
http://www.harnhst.demon.co.uk/ (Web-Page)

Havant (Council)
http://www.havant.gov.uk/ (Web-Page)

Health and Education Authority

http://www.hea.org.uk/ (Web-Page)

Health and Safety Executive
http://www.open.gov.uk/hse/hsehome.htm (Web-Page)

Health and Safety Laboratory
http://www.hsl.gov.uk/ (Web-Page)

Health, Department of
http://www.open.gov.uk/doh/tables96.htm (1995-1996 NHS Performance Guide)
http://www.ukpol.co.uk/dobson.htm (Dobson, Frank Secretary of State)
http://www.ukpol.co.uk/min.htm#hss (List of Health Cabinet Ministers this century)
http://www.open.gov.uk/doh/nhsest/hpage.htm (N.H.S. Estates)
http://www.coi.gov.uk/coi/depts/GDH/GDH.html (Press Releases)
http://www.open.gov.uk/doh/outlook.htm (Publications on the Internet)
http://www.open.gov.uk/doh/dhhome.htm (Web-Page)

Health Promotion Wales
http://www.hpw.org.uk/ (Web-Page)

Health Services Management Centre
http://www.bham.ac.uk/hsmc/ (Web-Page)

Heath, Edward (Former Prime Minister)
http://www-leland.stanford.edu/~cjacoby/heath.html (Demonisation of Edward Heath)

Henderson, Doug (Government Minister)
http://www.ukpol.co.uk/hen.htm (Biography)

Hereford and Worcester (Council)
http://www.open.gov.uk/hereford/home-page.htm (Web-Page)

Herefordshire (Council)
http://www.hereford-worcester.gov.uk/ (Web-Page)

Hertfordshire (Council)
http://www.hertscc.gov.uk/hcc/educatn/index.htm (Education)
http://www.hertscc.gov.uk/ (Web-Page)

HFEA
http://www.hfea.gov.uk/ (Web-Page)

Higher Education Funding Council For England
http://www.hefce.ac.uk/ (Web-Page)

Higher Education Statistics Agency
http://www.hesa.ac.uk/ (Web-Page)

Highways Agency
http://www.highways.gov.uk/ (Web-Page)

H.M. Customs and Excise (See also Customs)
http://www.hmce.gov.uk/ (Web-Page)

H.M.S.O.[NB, is now called just "The Stationery Office"]

http://www.the-stationery-office.co.uk/ (Web-Page)

H.M. Treasury (See also Treasury)
http://www.hm-treasury.gov.uk/ (Web-Page)

Hobbes, Thomas
gopher://gopher.vt.edu:10010/02/98/1 (Leviathan text)
http://swift.eng.ox.ac.uk/jdr/hobbes.html (Web-Page)

Hogg, Douglas (Former Agriculture Minister and MP)
http://www.ukpol.co.uk/hogg.htm (1996 Conservative Party Conference Speech)

Home Office
http://www.open.gov.uk/home_off/ho_funct.htm (Functions)
http://www.coi.gov.uk/coi/depts/GHO/GHO.html (Press Releases)
http://www.open.gov.uk/prison/prisonhm.htm (Prison Service)
http://www.open.gov.uk/pau/pauhome.htm (Public Appointments Unit)
http://www.open.gov.uk/home_off/rsdhome.htm (Research)
http://www.homeoffice.gov.uk/dob/index.htm (Responsibilities of Department)
http://www.homeoffice.gov.uk/hofront.htm (Web-Page)

Home Secretary (Currently Jack Straw)
http://www.ukpol.co.uk/min.htm#home (Historical List of Home Secretaries)
http://www.open.gov.uk/home_off/hofront.htm (Home Office Web-Page)
http://www.ukpol.co.uk/straw.htm (Jack Straw)

Hong Kong
http://www.fco.gov.uk/hongkong/index.html (Foreign Office Newsletter)
http://www.fco.gov.uk/hongkong/index.html (Web-Page)

Hoon, Geoff (Government Minister)
http://www.ukpol.co.uk/boon.htm (Biography)

Hounslow (Council)
http://www.hounslow.gov.uk/ (Web-Page)

House of Commons
http://www.open.gov.uk/commons/commons.htm (Business for the Week)
http://edm.ais.co.uk/ (Early Day Motions Database)
http://www.parliament.the-stationery-office.co.uk/pa/cm/cmhansrd.htm (Hansard)
http://www.locata.co.uk/commons (MP Locater)
http://www.parliament.the-stationery-office.co.uk/pa/cm/cmordpap.htm (Order Papers)
http://www.parliament.uk/commons/lib/pio.htm (Public Information Office)
http://www.parliament.the-stationery-office.co.uk/pa/cm/cmselect.htm (Select Committee Reports)
http://www.ukpol.co.uk/hou.htm (Terminology explained)

House of Lords
http://www.parliament.the-stationery-office.co.uk/pa/ld/ldhansrd.htm (Hansard)
http://www.parliament.the-stationery-office.co.uk/pa/ld/ldselinf.htm (Select Committees)
http://www.parliament.the-stationery-office.co.uk/pa/ld/ldhome.htm (Web-Page)

Houses of Parliament

http://www.ukpol.co.uk/hou.htm (Terminology explained)
http://www.parliament.uk/ (Web-Page)

Housing Corporation
http://www.demon.co.uk/hcorp (Web-Page

How to win a High School Election
http://www.schoolelection.com/ (Web-Page)

Howard, Michael (MP and Former Home Secretary)
http://www.penlex.org.uk/howard.html (Web-Page) (Unofficial)

Howell, Sir Ralph
http://www.unemployment.co.uk/ (Right-to-Work Scheme)

Hull (Council)
http://www.hullcc.gov.uk/ (Web-Page)

Human Fertilisation and Embryology Authority
http://www.hfea.gov.uk/ (Web-Page)

Hume, David
http://unix1.utm.edu/departments/phil/hume.html (Hume Archives)
http://www.oxy.edu/apa/hume.html (Hume Society)

Hunt Saboteurs Association
http://envirolink.org/arrs/HSA/features/joinleaf.html (About)
http://envirolink.org/arrs/HSA/cgi-bin/gentoc.cgi (Press Releases)
http://envirolink.org/arrs/HSA/hsa.html (Web-Page)

Hyndburn (Council)
http://www.hyndburnbc.gov.uk/ (Web-Page)

Immegration and Nationality
http://www.homeoffice.gov.uk/ind/hpg.htm (Web-Page)

Independent Commission on the Voting Scheme
http://www.votingcom.gov.uk/ (Web-Page)

Independent Labour Network
http://www.iln.labournet.org.uk (Web-Page)

Independent Television Commission
http://www.itc.org.uk/ (Web-Page)

Information Technology Services Agency
http://www.dss.gov.uk/itsa (Web-Page)

Inspectorate of Pollution
http://www.environment-agency.gov.uk/ (Web-Page)

Institute For Public Policy Research
http://www.ippr.org.uk/ (Web-Page)

Inter Governmental Conference (IGC)

http://www.europarl.eu.int/dg7/igc/en/pos-toc.htm (Position of all European Member States on the I.G.C.)

Internatinal Conservativre Group
http://www.come.to/icg (Web-Page)

International Development Department
http://www.dfid.gov.uk/ (Web-Page)

International Monetary Fund
http://www.imf.org/external/pubs/ft/ar/imf.htm (1996 Annual Report)
http://www.imf.org/external/about.htm (About the I.M.F.)
http://www.imf.org/external/pubs/ft/survey/sup0996/14chrono.htm (Chronology)
http://www.imf.org/external/pubs/ft/pam/pam45/contents.htm (Financial Position)
http://www.imf.org/ (Web-Page)
http://www.imf.org/external/pubs/ft/exrp/differ/differ.htm (World Bank and the IMF)

International Socialist Group
http://www.tcp.co.uk/~johnboss/isg/ (Web-Page)

International Third Position
http://dspace.dial.pipex.com/town/plaza/rbg93/ (Web-Page)

Intervention Board
http://www.open.gov.uk/ib/ibdoes.htm (About Intervention Board)
http://www.open.gov.uk/ib/ibhome.htm (Web-Page)

Invest In Britain Bureau
http://www.dti.gov.uk/ibb/ (Web-Page)

Ipswich (Council)
http://www.ukpol.co.uk/ipswich.htm (1996 Local Election Results for Ipswich BC)
http://www.ukpol.co.uk/nlfm.htm#I (Previous party make-up for Ipswich BC)
http://www.ipswich.gov.uk/ (Web-Page)

Islamic Party of Britain
http://www.muslims.net/islamparty/islamparty.htm (Web-Page)

Isle of Man (Council)
http://www.gov.im/ (Web-Page)

Isle of Man Parlaiment
http://www.tynwald.isle-of-man.org.im/ (Web-Page)

Isle of Wight (Council)
http://www.wightonline.co.uk (Web-Page)

Islington (Council)
http://www.islington.gov.uk/council/ (Web-Page)

I.T For All
http://www.itforall.gov.uk/it/home/index.htm (Web-Page)

Ivor Peska's Politics Page
http://www.club.demon.co.uk/ (Web-Page)

Jersey
http://www.jersey.gov.uk/ (Web-Page)

Joint Declaration of Peace
http://www.bess.tcd.ie/dclrtn.htm (Text)

Joint Nature Conservation Committee
http://www.jncc.gov.uk/ (Web-Page)

Kable
http://www.kable.co.uk/ (Web-Page)

Kent (Council)
http://www.rmplc.co.uk/eduweb/sites/kentlea/index.html (Education)
http://www.kent.gov.uk/ (Web-Page)

Kingston-Upon-Hull (Council)
http://www.open.gov.uk/hullcc/index.htm (Web-Page)

Kinnock, Neil (Former Labour Leader)
http://www.ukpol.co.uk/kinnock.htm (Biography)

Kirklees (Council)
http://www.hud.ac.uk/local/kitp/kmcedu.html (Web-Page)

Knitwear and Footwear Union
http://www.poptel.org.uk/kfat/ (Web-Page)

Knowsley (Council)
http://www.connect.org.uk/merseyworld/knowsley_mb/ (Web-Page)

Labour Party
http://www.ukpol.co.uk/lpl.htm (List of 20th Century Leaders)
http://www.aber.ac.uk/~scty11/ (Aberystwyth University Labour Club)
http://politicsgovernment.321media.com/adlc.htm (Association of Democratic Labour Clubs)
http://www.bath.ac.uk/~su2lsa/home.html (Bath Labour Students)
http://www.cam.ac.uk/CambUniv/Societies/cols/ (Cambridge University Labour Students)
http://www.ukpol.co.uk/boo2.htm (Complete list of Labour candidates at 1997 election)
http://www.mic.dundee.ac.uk/dusa/soc18.html (Dundee University Labour Association)
http://www.dur.ac.uk/~dds8lc (Durham University Labour Club)
http://www.ed.ac.uk/~labour/ (Edinburgh University Labour Club)
http://www.eplp.org.uk/ (European Parliamentary Labour Party)
http://www.cplab.ph.ed.ac.uk/~jfa/fyl.html (Falkirk Young Labour)
http://www.islington.org.uk/labour/ (Islington South Labour Party)
http://www.poptel.org.uk/labour-party/eplp/name.html (List of Labour MEPs)
http://www.yi.com/home/MaidstonelabourParty/ (Maidstone Labour Party)
http://www.personal.u-net.com/~upnorth/labour.htm (Manchester Uni Labour Club)
http://www.ukpol.co.uk/labf.htm (Membership)
http://www.poptel.org.uk/regeneration/ (Regeneration/Labour Youth)
http://www.shef.ac.uk:80/uni/projects/sfl/ (Scientists for Labour)
http://www.shef.ac.uk/~lc/labour.html (Sheffield Labour Students)
http://www2.poptel.org.uk/slp/ (Southampton Labour Party)

http://www.poptel.org.uk/stockport-labour/ (Stockport Labour Group)
http://web-site.lineone.net/~sotlabour/ (Stoke-on-Trent Labour Party)
http://webzone1.co.uk/www/trafflabgrp/traflab1.htm (Trafford Labour Group)
http://www.labour.org.uk/ (Web-Page)
http://www.geocities.com/CapitolHill/1374/ (Wythenshawe and Sale East Labour)
http://www.york.ac.uk/~socs138/ (York University Labour Association)

Labour Euro Safeguards Campaign
http://www.lesc.org.uk/ (Web-Page)

Labour Left Briefing
http://www.llb.labournet.org.uk/ (Web-Page)

Labour Reform
http://www.cix.co.uk/~ecotrend/LR/ (Web-Page)

Labour Research Department
http://www.lrd.org.uk/ (Web-Page)

Labournet
http://www.labournet.org.uk (Web-Page)

Lancashire (Council)
http://www.lancashire.com/lcc/lccindex.htm (Web-Page)

League Against Cruel Sports
http://Lightman.co.uk/lacs/press/index.html (Press Releases)
http://Lightman.co.uk/lacs/ (Web-Page)

Leeds (Council)
http://www.leeds.gov.uk/lcc/lcc.html (Council Information)
http://www.leeds.gov.uk/lcc/cncllrs/a-m.html (Councillors)
http://www.leeds.gov.uk/lcc/cncllrs/electmap.html (Election Map)
http://www.keele.ac.uk/depts/po/table/brit/lee.htm (Election Results for May 1996)
http://www.leeds.gov.uk/ (Web-Pages)

Legal Aid
http://www.open.gov.uk/lab/legal.htm (Web-Page)

Lagal System
http://www.uni-wuerzburg.de/law/uk__indx.html (Guide to British Legal System)

Lewisham (Council)
http://www.lewisham.gov.uk/howrun.html (Council)
http://www.lewisham.gov.uk/depts/education/edindex.htm (Education)
http://www.lewisham.gov.uk/ (Web-Page)

Liberal Democrat Party
http://www.libdems.org.uk/ (Web-Page)
http://www.compulink.co.uk/~broadway/index.html (Aylesbury Liberal Democrats)
http://www.kbnet.co.uk/liberal democrat (Bedford and Kempston Liberal Democrats)
http://www.gold.net/users/fu30/libdems.htm (Cambridge Liberal Democrats)
http://www.compulink.co.uk/~catbells/csld/ (Cambridge Student Liberal Democrats)

http://www.ukpol.co.uk/boo2.htm (Complete list of 1997 Liberal Democrats candidates)
http://www.geocities.com/CapitolHill/1334/ (Didsbury Ward (Liverpool) Lib Democrats)
http://www.ed.ac.uk/~libdems/ (Edinburgh Student Liberal Democrats)
http://www.libdems.org.uk/history/history.htm (History)
http://www.le.ac.uk/CWIS/SU/SO/LDSOC/ldsoc.html (Leicester Student Liberal Dems)
http://www.libdems.org.uk/directry/england.htm (List of Councillors)
http://www.libdems.org.uk/directry/eu.htm (List of MEPs)
http://www.libdems.org.uk/directry/ukparl.htm (List of MPs)
http://www.ncl.ac.uk/~n5017831/lib.html (Newcastle Student Liberal Democrats)
http://info.ox.ac.uk/~newc0247/Liberal Democrat/ (Oxford Student Liberal Democrats)
http://www.libdems.org.uk/policy/mainpol.htm (Policies)
http://www.scotlibdems.org.uk/index.htm (Scottish Liberal Democrats)
http://www.scotlibdems.org.uk/ao/syld/clubs.htm (Scottish Young Lib Democrats)
http://www.cix.co.uk/~stratfordlibdems/welcome.htm (Stratford and South Warwickshire Liberal Democrats)
http://www.ucl.ac.uk/~uczxlib/ (UCL Liberal Democrats)
http://www.lookup.com/Homepages/53514/home.html (West Wiltshire Liberal Dems)
http://ourworld.compuserve.com/homepages/gmorris/wwlibdem.htm (West Worcestershire Liberal Democrats)
http://www.cix.co.uk/~liberal democrat-woodspring/ (Woodspring Liberal Democrats)
http://www.yardley.libdems.org.uk/ (Yardley Liberal Democrats)

Liberal Party
http://www.zem.co.uk/oflib/index.htm (Offmore and Comberton Liberals)
http://www.libparty.demon.co.uk/ (Web-Page)

libertarian Allience
http://www.digiweb.com/igeldard/LA/economic.htm (Economic Publications)
http://www.digiweb.com/igeldard/LA/philosophical.htm (Philosophical Publications)
http://www.digiweb.com/igeldard/LA/political.htm (Political Publications)
http://www.digiweb.com/igeldard/LA/ (Web-Page)

Liberator Magazine
http://www.liberator.org.uk/ (Web-Page)
http://www.liberator.org.uk/collect.htm (About Liberator)

Libraries
http://portico.bl.uk/ (British Library)
http://www.bubl.ac.uk/link/a/academiclibrariesinengland.htm (University Libraries)

lincolnshire (Council)
http://www.personal.u-net.com/~lincscc/lcc.htm (Council Information)
http://www.personal.u-net.com/~lincscc/ (Web-Page)

Liverpool (Council)
http://www.connect.org.uk/liv_council/public/council_info/anrep/anrep-index.html (Annual Report of Council)
http://www.connect.org.uk/liv_council/public/council_info/infomain.html (Council Information)
http://www.connect.org.uk/liv_council/public/council_info/wardinfo/wards.html (Ward and Councillors)

http://www.connect.org.uk/liv_council/public/ (Web-Page)

Lloyd George
http://www.ukpol.co.uk/llgeorge.jpg (Picture)

Lloyd, Tony (Government Minister)
http://www.ukpol.co.uk/lloyd.htm (Biography)

Lobster MagazineLOBSTER MAGAZINE:
http://www.knowledge.co.uk/xxx/lobster/ (Web-Page)

Local Elections
http://www.warwick.ac.uk/~suaba/Politics/Elections/loc95eng.html (1995 English Local Election Results
http://www.warwick.ac.uk/~suaba/Politics/Elections/loc95sco.html (1995 Scottish Local Election Results)
http://www.warwick.ac.uk/~suaba/Politics/Elections/loc95wal.html (1995 Welsh Local Election Results)
http://www.ukpol.co.uk/loca.htm (1996 English Local Election Results)
http://www.ukpol.co.uk/loca.htm (1997 County Council Elections)
http://www.ukpol.co.uk/byer.htm (Summary of 1995 local by-elections)
http://www.ukpol.co.uk/byte.htm (Results of local by-elections since 1995)

Local Government
http://www.oultwood.com/localgov/index.htm (Charles Sale's Links Page)
http://www.oultwood.com/localgov/nowebsite.htm (Councils Without Web-Sites)
http://www.ukpol.co.uk/coun.htm (Local Councils with Web-Pages)
http://www.open.gov.uk/doe/lgfp/index.htm (Local Government Finance)
http://www.open.gov.uk/doe/lgfp/flas/keystats.htm (Local Government Finance Statistics)
http://www.local.gov.uk/ (Official Site)

Local Government Association
http://www.lga.gov.uk/ (Web-Page)

Local Government Information Unit
http://www.lglu.gov.uk/ (Web-Page)

Locke, John
http://swift.eng.ox.ac.uk/jdr/locke.html (Web-Page)

London Class War
http://www.geocities.com/CapitolHill/9482/lc4098.htm (Web-Page)

Lord Chancellors Department
http://www.open.gov.uk/lcd/lcdhome.htm (Web-Page)

Low Pay Commission
http://www.lowpay.gov.uk/ (Web-Page)

Luton (Council)
http://www.luton.gov.uk/ (Web-Page)

Magazines and Newspapers
http://ourworld.compuserve.com/homepages/TheCitizen/ (Citizen)

http://www.cnn.com/ (C.N.N.)
http://www.economist.com/index.htm (Economist Magazine)
http://envirolink.org/arrs/LACS/ewg1_idx.htm (Electronic Wildlife (LACS))
http://www.gold.net/flames/pl.html (Flames Magazine)
http://www.conwayfor.org/forward.html (Forward Magazine)
http://www.futurenet.com/ (Futurenet News)(Requires Free Registration)
http://www.liberator.org.uk/ (Liberator Magazine)
http://www.junius.co.uk/ (Living Marxism)
http://www.knowledge.co.uk/xxx/lobster/ (Lobster Magazine)
http://www.poptel.org.uk/morning-star/ (Morning Star)
http://www.newscientist.com/ (New Scientist)
http://freespace.virgin.net/i.nicol/op.html (Open Polemic)
http://ourworld.compuserve.com/homepages/rebellion (Rebellion)
http://www.gn.apc.org/demleft/ (Red Kite)
http://www.demon.co.uk/xyz/Scallywag/index.html (Scallywag)
http://www.sunday-times.co.uk/ (Sunday Times, requires free registration)
http://www.thetablet.co.uk/ (The Times, requires free registration)
http://www.users.dircon.co.uk/~thirdway/files/1stindex.html (Third Way)
http://www.abel.co.uk/~rost2000/tribune (Tribune Newspaper)
http://www.netlink.co.uk/users/natdems/vag0intr.htm (Vanguard)

M.A.F.F. (Ministry of Agriculture, Fisheries and Food):
http://www.maff.gov.uk/aboutmaf/maffindx.htm (About MAFF)
http://www.maff.gov.uk/animalh/bse/bseindx.htm (B.S.E. Information Page)

Magna Carta
http://portico.bl.uk/access/treasures/magna-carta.html (Web-Page)

Major, John (Former Prime Minister)
http://www.ukpol.co.uk/aaa.htm (Biography)
http://www.conservative-party.org.uk/newspags/1-96.htm (New Year Message)
http://www.purple.co.uk/purplet/conserv/majorsp1.htm (Resignation Speech)

Majority
http://www.ukpol.co.uk/low.htm (Smallest % share of a vote for a winning MP)

Malvern Hills (Council)
http://www.open.gov.uk/hereford/pages/malvdc2.htm (Council Information)
http://www.open.gov.uk/hereford/pages/mhdchome.htm (Web-Page)

Manchester (Council)
http://www.manchester.gov.uk/cllrs/index.htm (Councillors)
http://www.poptel.org.uk/infosource/atoz.html (Guide to Council Services)
http://www.manchester.gov.uk/ (Web-Page)

Mandelson, Peter (Former Government Cabinet Minister)
http://www.ukpol.co.uk/mandel.htm (Biography)

Manifestos
1945:
http://www.ukpol.co.uk/con45.htm (Conservative Party Manifesto)
http://www.ukpol.co.uk/lab45.htm (Labour Party Manifesto)

http://www.ukpol.co.uk/lib45.htm (Liberal Party Manifesto)
1950:
http://www.ukpol.co.uk/con50.htm (Conservative Party Manifesto)
http://www.ukpol.co.uk/lab50.htm (Labour Party Manifesto)
http://www.ukpol.co.uk/lib50.htm (Liberal Party Manifesto)
1951:
http://www.ukpol.co.uk/con51.htm (Conservative Party Manifesto)
http://www.ukpol.co.uk/lab51.htm (Labour Party Manifesto)
http://www.ukpol.co.uk/lib51.htm (Liberal Party Manifesto)
1955:
http://www.ukpol.co.uk/con55.htm (Conservative Party Manifesto)
http://www.ukpol.co.uk/lab55.htm (Labour Party Manifesto)
http://www.ukpol.co.uk/lib55.htm (Liberal Party Manifesto)
1959:
http://www.ukpol.co.uk/con59.htm (Conservative Party Manifesto)
http://www.ukpol.co.uk/lab59.htm (Labour Party Manifesto)
http://www.ukpol.co.uk/lib59.htm (Liberal Party Manifesto)
1964:
http://www.ukpol.co.uk/con64.htm (Conservative Party Manifesto)
http://www.ukpol.co.uk/lab64.htm (Labour Party Manifesto)
http://www.ukpol.co.uk/lib64.htm (Liberal Party Manifesto)
1966:
http://www.ukpol.co.uk/con66.htm (Conservative Party Manifesto)
http://www.ukpol.co.uk/lab66.htm (Labour Party Manifesto)
http://www.ukpol.co.uk/lib66.htm (Liberal Party Manifesto)
1970:
http://www.ukpol.co.uk/con70.htm (Conservative Party Manifesto)
http://www.ukpol.co.uk/lab70.htm (Labour Party Manifesto)
http://www.ukpol.co.uk/lib70.htm (Liberal Party Manifesto)
1974: (February)
http://www.ukpol.co.uk/con74feb.htm (Conservative Party Manifesto)
http://www.ukpol.co.uk/lab74feb.htm (Labour Party Manifesto)
http://www.ukpol.co.uk/lib74feb.htm (Liberal Party Manifesto)
1974: (October)
http://www.ukpol.co.uk/con74oct.htm (Conservative Party Manifesto)
http://www.ukpol.co.uk/lab74oct.htm (Labour Party Manifesto)
http://www.ukpol.co.uk/lib74oct.htm (Liberal Party Manifesto)
1979:
http://www.ukpol.co.uk/con79.htm (Conservative Party Manifesto)
http://www.ukpol.co.uk/lab79.htm (Labour Party Manifesto)
http://www.ukpol.co.uk/lib79.htm (Liberal Party Manifesto)
1983:
http://www.ukpol.co.uk/con83.htm (Conservative Party Manifesto)
http://www.ukpol.co.uk/lab83.htm (Labour Party Manifesto)
http://www.ukpol.co.uk/all83.htm (Liberal-SDP Alliance Manifesto)
1987:
http://www.ukpol.co.uk/con87.htm (Conservative Party Manifesto)
http://www.ukpol.co.uk/lab87.htm (Labour Party Manifesto)

http://www.ukpol.co.uk/lib87.htm (Liberal-SDP Alliance Party Manifesto)
1992:
http://www.ukpol.co.uk/con92.htm (Conservative Party Manifesto)
http://www.ukpol.co.uk/lab92.htm (Labour Party Manifesto)
1997:
http://www.ukpol.co.uk/ge97.htm (List of 1997 manifestos)

Manuil (Celtic National Party):
http://www.awod.com/gallery/rwav/robertg/manuil.html (Web-Page)

Meat and Hygiene Service
http://www.maff.gov.uk/aboutmaf/agency/mhs.htm (Web-Page)

Mebyon Kernow
http://www.btinternet.com/~cornishman/ (Web-Page)

Media UK
http://www.mediauk.com/ (Web-Page)

Members of Parliament
http://www.gn.apc.org/myvote/ (Addresses for all M.P.s and P.P.C.s)
http://www.ukpol.co.uk/email.htm (E-mail addresses for M.P.s)
http://www.conservative-party.org.uk/mpsname/mpsname.htm (List of Conservative MPs)
http://www.libdems.org.uk/directry/ukparl.htm (List of Liberal Democrat MPs)
http://www.qmw.ac.uk/~laws/election/allbritmp.html (List of MPs)
http://www.ukpol.co.uk/den.htm (MPs deselected 1970-1996)
http://www.ukpol.co.uk/other.htm (New Tory candidates standing at the next General Election)
http://www.gn.apc.org/myvote/ (Search for your MP by postcode)
http://www.ukpol.co.uk/selfish.htm (Who voted for Pay-Rises in July 1996?)
http://www.ukpol.co.uk/small.htm (With Majorities of under 500)

Members of the European Parliament (British)
http://www.ip7.co.uk/beacon-tory/mep.htm (Elles, James. Conservative)
http://www.mel-read.org.uk/ (Read, Mel)
http://www.poptel.org.uk/john.tomlinson/ (Tomlinson, John. Birmingham West. Labour)
http://www.poptel.org.uk/carole-tongue/ (Tongue, Carole. London East)

Members of Parliament and P.P.C.s With Web Pages
http://www.labour.org.uk/plp/graham.allen/index.html (Allen, Graham. Nottingham North. Labour MP)
http://www.home.co.uk/dblunkettmp/ (Blunkett, David. Sheffield Brightside.Labour MP)
http://www.compulink.co.uk/~broadway/ald/biog.html (Bowles, Sharon. Aylesbury. Liberal Democrat PPC)
http://www.scotlibdems.org.uk/lp/gordon/mp.htm (Bruce, Malcolm. Gordon. Lib Dem MP)
http://www.compulink.co.uk/~icph/cable.htm (Cable, Vince. Liberal Democrat PPC. : Twickenham)
http://www.worldserver.pipex.com/anne.campbell/ (Campbell, Anne. Cambridge. Labour MP)
http://www1.btwebworld.com/markcampbell/ (Campbell, Mark. Labour PPC Suffolk Coastal)

http://www.scotlibdems.org.uk/lp/nefife/mp.htm (Campbell, Menzies. North East Fife. Lib Dem MP)

http://dspace.dial.pipex.com/town/square/hi13/ (Evans, Nigel. Ribble Valley. Conservative MP)

http://www.solnet.co.uk/fabricant/ (Fabricant, Michael Lichfield. Conservative MP)

http://www.netlink.co.uk/users/shaw/tim.html (Kirkhope, Tim. Leeds NE. Conservative MP)

http://www.poptel.org.uk/ken-livingstone (Livingstone,Ken. Brent East. Labour)

http://www.margaretmoran.org/ (Moran, Margaret. Luton South. Labour MP)

http://www.lewisham.gov.uk/mps/prentice.html (Prentice, Bridget. Lewisham East. Labour MP)

http://www.netlink.co.uk/users/shaw/ (Shaw, David. Dover. Former Conservative MP)

http://www.islington.org.uk/labour/chris (Smith, Chris. Labour MP. Islington South)

http://www.users.zetnet.co.uk/pcrrn/steinberg/ (Steinberg, Gerry. Durham. Labour MP)

http://www.onid.com/labour.mp/stimms/ (Timms, Stephen. Newham North-East. Labour MP)

http://www.nwh-tories.org.uk/george01.htm (Young, Sir George. Conservative MP)

Members of Parliament With Web Pages About Them
http://www.penlex.org.uk/howard.html (Howard, Michael)
http://www.penlex.org.uk/widdecom.html (Widdecombe, Ann)

Mendip (Council)
http://www.mendip.gov.uk/ (Web-Page)

Metropolitan Police
http://www.open.gov.uk/police/mps/mps/mis/mps-indx.htm (Index)
http://www.open.gov.uk/police/mps/home.htm (Web-Page)

Militant Labour
http://homepages.enterprise.net/mcmillan/militant.html (Militant Teacher)
http://www.i-way.co.uk/~militant/ (Reading and Oxford Branch)
http://www.i-way.co.uk/~militant/ysr.html (Reading and Oxford Youth Branch)
http://members.tripod.com/~militant/Reclaim_the_Game (Taking money out of football)

Militant Teacher
http://homepages.enterprise.net/mcmillan/militant.html (Web-Page)

Mill, John Stuart
http://www.ukpol.co.uk/gopher://wiretap.spies.com/00/Library/Classic/liberty.jsm (On Liberty)
http://www.ukpol.co.uk/gopher://gopher.vt.edu:10010/02/122/2 (Representative Government Text)
http://www.ukpol.co.uk/gopher://gopher.vt.edu:10010/02/122/3 (Utilitarianism Text)
http://swift.eng.ox.ac.uk/jdr/mill.html (Web-Page)

Millenium Commission
http://www.millennium.gov.uk/ (Web-Page)

Milton Keynes
http://ourworld.compuserve.com/homepages/gareth_lewis/ (Web-Page)

Mitchell Commission

http://www.unite.net/customers/alliance/Mitchellrep.html (Mitchell Commission Report)

Monarchist League
http://www.geocities.com/Athens/7993/ (Web-Page)

Monarchy
http://www.royal.gov.uk/start.htm (Diana Memorial Pages)
http://www.britannia.com/history/h6.html (History)
http://www.royal.gov.uk/history/index.htm (History)
http://www.royal.gov.uk/collect/index.htm (Royal Collection)
http://www.royal.gov.uk/palaces/index.htm (Royal Palaces)
http://www.itl.net/features/camelot/royal/royals.html (Web-Page)
http://www.neosoft.com/~dlgates/uk/ukspecific.html?pix_windsors (Web-Page)
http://www.royal.gov.uk/ (Web-Page - Official)

Monopolies and Mergers Commission
http://www.open.gov.uk/mmc/mmchome.htm (Web-Page)

Monster Raving Loony party
http://www.raving-loony.pv.org/ (Web-Page)

More, Sir Thomas
gopher://wiretap.spies.com:70/00/Library/Classic/utopia.txt (Text of Utopia)

Morning Star
http://www.poptel.org.uk/morning-star/ (Web-Page)

Motions of No Confidence
http://www.ukpol.co.uk/noc.htm (M of NC since 1976)

Movement For Middle England
http://www.netcomuk.co.uk/~mullaney/title.htm (Web-Page)

National Audit Office
http://www.open.gov.uk/nao/annual.htm (Annual Report)
http://www.open.gov.uk/nao/subject.htm (List of Reports)
http://www.open.gov.uk/nao/home.htm (Web-Page)

National Criminal Intelligence Unit
http://www.open.gov.uk/ncis/ncishome.htm (Web-Page)

National Curriculum
http://www.dfee.gov.uk/nc/ (Web-Page)

National Democrats
http://www.netlink.co.uk/users/natdems/ (Web-Page)
http://www.netlink.co.uk/users/natdems/intro.htm (Policies)
http://www.netlink.co.uk/cgi-crystalx/chartfrm (Political Profiler
http://www.netlink.co.uk/users/natdems/vag0intr.htm (Vanguard

National Front
http://www.national-front.org.uk (Web-Page)

National Grid For Learning

http://www.ngfl.gov.uk/ (Web-Page)

National Health Service
(See under Department of Health)

National Heritage
http://www.nhm.ac.uk/ (Natural History Museum)
http://www.heritage.gov.uk/WORK.HTM (Policies)
http://www.coi.gov.uk/coi/depts/GHE/GHE.html (Press Releases)
http://www.heritage.gov.uk/ (Web-Page)

National Lottery
http://www.millennium.gov.uk/ (Millennium Commission)
http://www.nlcb.org.uk/ (National Lottery Charities Board)
http://www.lottery.culture.gov.uk/ (Web-Page)

National Savings
http://www.open.gov.uk/natsva/nshome.htm (Web-Page)

National Secular Society
http://secularism.org.uk/ (Web-Page)

National Union of Students (N.U.S.)
http://www.nus.org.uk/fsate.html (Funding Students)
http://www.nus.org.uk/ (Web-Page)

NATO (North Atlantic Treaty Organisation)
http://www.nato.int/ (Web-Page)

Natural Law Party
http://www.natural-law-party.org.uk/ (Web-Page)
http://www.personal.u-net.com/~natlaw/policy.htm (Policies.)

Natural Law Party, Northern Ireland
http://there.is/natural-law-party-NI/ (Web-Page)

National Association of Citizens Advice Bureaux
http://www.nacab.org.uk/ (Web-Page)

National Libraries
http://portico.bl.uk/ (British Library)
http://www.nls.uk/ (National Library of Scotland)
http://www.llgc.org.uk/ (National Library of Wales)

National Lottery
http://www.lottery.culture.gov.uk/ (Web-Page)

New Allience
http://www.users.dircon.co.uk/~iits/newalliance (Web-Page)

New Britain
http://web.on-line.co.uk/stuart.n2/nbrit.html (Web-Page)

New Britain, New Ideas
http://www.geocities.com/CapitolHill/7081/ (Web-Page)

Newbury (Council)
http://www.newburydc.gov.uk/ (Web-Page)

Nebury By-Pass Campaign
http://gnew.gn.apc.org/newbury/ (Web-Page)

Newcastle (Council)
http://www.newcastle-city-council.gov.uk/ (Web-Page)

Newcastle -Under-Lyme (Council)
http://www.cityscape.co.uk/users/bd90/council.htm Borough Council (Web-Page)

New Communist Party
http://www.geocities.com/CapitolHill/2853/ (Web-Page)

New Deal
http://www.newdeal.gov.uk/ (Web-Page)

Newham (Council)
http://www.newham.gov.uk/ (Web-Page)

Newport (Council)
http://www.newport.gov.uk/ (Web-Page)

News
http://www.ukpol.co.uk/news.htm (Latest political and electoral news)
See under the #mag Magazines and News Section

New Titles
http://www.poptel.org.uk/demleft/newtimes/ (Web-Page)

Newtownards (Council)
http://www.nics.gov.uk/geninfo/nitb/n_ards.htm (Web-Page)

Nexus
http://www.netnexus.org/ (Web-Page)

Nicholas Whyte's Northern Ireland Resources
http://explorers.whyte.com/ (Web-Page)

No Confidence Motions
http://www.ukpol.co.uk/noc.htm (Since 1976)

Nolan Committee
http://www.open.gov.uk/nolan/csplhome.htm (Web-Page)
http://www.the-stationery-office.co.uk/document/parliament/nolan3/nolan.htm (Summary of Third Report.)
http://www.coi.gov.uk/coi/depts/GPL/GPL.html (Press Releases)

Non-Departmental Public Bodies (Quangos)
http://www.open.gov.uk/co/publicbo.htm (Government Web-Page)

North Atlantic Treaty Organisation (N.A.T.O.)
http://www.ukpol.co.uk/gopher://marvin.stc.nato.int:70/11/yugo (Web-Page)

Norfolk County Council
http://www.norfolk.gov.uk/ (Web-Page)

North Hertfordshire (Council)
http://www.cityscape.co.uk/users/ag60/ (Web-Page)

North Wiltshire (Council)
http://www.hiway.co.uk/nwilts/ (Web-Page)

Northern Ireland
http://explorers.whyte.com/ (1998 Assembly Elections from Nicholas Whyte)
http://www.dedni.gov.uk/ (Department of Economic Development for Northern Ireland)
http://www.unite.net/customers/alliance/elfull.html (Election Results)
http://www.nics.gov.uk/centgov/nio/framewrk.htm (Framework Document)
http://www.ukpol.co.uk/irish.htm (Irish Politics Page)
http://www.bess.tcd.ie/dclrtn.htm (Joint Declaration of Peace)
http://www.unite.net/customers/alliance/Mitchellrep.html (Mitchell Commission Report)
http://indigo.ie/~saoirse/record.htm (Latest news from Republican SF)
http://explorers.whyte.com/ (Nicholas Whyte's Web-Page)
http://www.ni-assembly.gov.uk/ (Northern Ireland Assembly)
http://www.nics.gov.uk/ (Northern Ireland Government Server)
http://www.nio.gov.uk/ (Northern Ireland Office)
http://www.unite.net/customers/alliance/forum.html (Peace Forum)
http://www.ulst.ac.uk/services/library/ni/nitime.htm (Time-Line and History of Northern Ireland)
http://www.uup.org/text/current/c_fire.html (Ulster Unionists Reaction to end of Cease-Fire)

Northern Ireland Assembly
http://www.ni-assembly.gov.uk/ (Web-Page)

Northumberland (Council)
http://nw.demon.co.uk/northumberland/ (Web-Page)

Norwich (Council)
http://www.norwich.gov.uk/ (Web-Page)

Nottinghamshire (Council)
http://www.nottscc.gov.uk/ (Web-Page, Requires Frames)

Nursary Vouchers
http://homepages.enterprise.net/mcmillan/vouchers.html (Article against nursery vouchers)

OFFER (Electricity Regulator)
http://www.open.gov.uk/offer/offerhm.htm (Web-Page)

Office For National Statistics
http://www.ons.gov.uk/ (Web-Page)

Office of Fair Trading
http://www.oft.gov.uk/ (Web-Page)

Office of Science and Technology
http://www.dti.gov.uk/ost/ (Web-Page)

OFGAS (Gas Regulator)
http://www.ofgas.gov.uk/ (Web-Page)

OFSTED (Education Regulator)
http://www.ofsted.gov.uk/ (Web-Page)

OFTEL (Telecommunications Regulator)
http://wwww.oftel.gov.uk/ (Web-Page)

OFWAT (Water Regulator)
http://www.open.gov.uk/ofwat/index.htm (Web-Page)

Open Polemic
http://freespace.virgin.net/i.nicol/op.html (Web-Page)

Opinion Polls
http://www.gallup.com/ (Gallup)
http://www.ukpol.co.uk/polls.htm (1997 Polls Information)
The above page has links to opinion poll results since 1945.

Ordnance Survey
http://www.ordsvy.co.uk/ (Web-Page)

ORR (Rail Regulator)
http://www.rail-reg.gov.uk/

Other Political Links Sites
http://dspace.dial.pipex.com/town/avenue/pn72/ (PJW's British Politics Web Site)

Oxford (Council)
http://www.i-way.co.uk/oxcity/councillors/council.html (Councillors)
http://www.i-way.co.uk/oxcity/ (Web-Page)

Oxfordshire (Council)
http://www.open.gov.uk/oxcis/html/1017/F84DC.1 (Council Information)
http://www.open.gov.uk/oxcis/html/1017/18D44.1 (Web-Page)

PAMIS
http://www.pamis.gov.uk/ (Web-Page)

Parliament
See also under House of Commons and House of Lords
http://www.parliament.uk/lib/fact.htm (Factsheets)
http://www.publications.hmso.gov.uk/hmso/publicat/hmsopinf.htm (Parliamentary Productions) (from SO)
http://www.ukpol.co.uk/hou.htm (Terminology explained)
http://www.parliament.uk/lib/viasci.htm (Tours around Parliament)
http://www.parliament.uk/ (Web-Page)
http://www.parliament.uk/parliament/edunit.htm (UK Parliament Education Unit)

Parliamentary Channel

http://www.parlchan.co.uk/ (Web-Page)

Parliamentary Commissioner For Administration
http://www.ombudsman.org.uk/ (Web-Page)

Passport Agency
http://www.open.gov.uk/ukpass/ukpass.htm (Web-Page)

Patent Office
http://www.patent.gov.uk/ (Web-Page)

Pembrokeshire (Council)
http://www.pembrokeshire.gov.uk/ (Web-Page)

Penal Lexicon
http://www.penlex.org.uk/index.html (Web-Page)

Pensions Advisory Service
http://www.opas.org.uk/ (Web-Page)

Plaid Cymru
http://www.btinternet.com/~ws/plaid/index-s.html (Aberystwyth University)
http://freespace.virgin.net/adam.rykala (Blaneau Gwent)
http://www.plaid.freeserve.co.uk/ (Cardiff South)
http://ceredigion.plaidcymru.org/ (Ceredigion)
http://www.btinternet.com/~ws/plaid/index-s.html (Federation of Plaid Cymru Students)
http://www.wales.com/political-party/plaid-cymru/policies/policies.html (Policies)
http://www.plaid-cymru.wales.com/pontypridd (Pontypridd)
http://www.plaid-cymru.wales.com/ (Web-Page)

Planning Inspectorate
http://www.open.gov.uk/pi/pihome.htm (Web-Page)

Plymouth (Council)
http://www.plymouth.gov.uk/1300000.htm (Council Information)
http://www.plymouth.gov.uk/ (Web-Page)

Police
http://www.pfed.demon.co.uk/ (Police Federation)
http://www.police.uk/ (Police Service)
http://www.ruc.police.uk/ (Royal Ulster Constabulary)

Police Federation
http://www.pfed.demon.co.uk/ (Web-Page)

Political Parties (See also under individual names)
http://www.conservative-party.org.uk/ (Conservative Party)
http://www.labour.org.uk/ (Labour Party)
http://www.libdems.org.uk/ (Liberal Democrats)
http://www.plaidcyrmu.org/ (Plaid Cymru)
http://www.snp.org.uk/ (Scottish National Party)
http://www.ukpol.co.uk/party.htm (Size of Parliamentary Parties 1979-1996)

Political Science Resources

164

http://www.psr.keele.ac.uk/ (Web-Page)

Politico's Bookstore & Coffee House
http://www.politicos.co.uk/ (Web-Page)

Politico's Publishing
http://www.politicos.co.uk/publ.htm (Web-Page)

Post Office
http://www.parcelforce.com/ (Parcelforce)
http://www.postoffice-counters.com/ (Post Office Counters)
http://www.royalmail.com/ (Royal Mail)
http://www.postoffice.co.uk/ (Web-Page)

Powys (Council)
http://www.powys.gov.uk/pcc/counclrs.htm (County Councillors)
http://www.powys.gov.uk/pcc/pcc.htm (General Information)
http://www.powys.gov.uk/default.htm (Web-Page)

Prescott, John (Deputy Prime Minister)
http://www.ukpol.co.uk/prescott.htm (Biography)

Press Complaints Commission
http://www.pcc.org.uk/ (Press Complaints Commission)

Prime Minister
http://www.ukpol.co.uk/pm.htm (List of all Prime Ministers since 1721)
http://www.ukpol.co.uk/prime.htm (Information about Prime Ministers since 1945.)
http://www.number-10.gov.uk/ Official (10 Downing Street, Web-Page)

Prince of Wales
http://www.fco.gov.uk/reference/biographies/princecharles_english.html (Foreign Office Web-Page)
http://www.princes-trust.org.uk/ (Web-Page)

Prisons
http://www.penlex.org.uk/index.html (Penal Lexicon)
http://www.ukpol.co.uk/pri.htm (Prison Populations 1900-1990)
http://www.open.gov.uk/prison/prisonhm.htm (Prison Service)
http://www.penlex.org.uk/ps95repo.html (Prison Service Annual Report 1994-1995)

Private Finance Initiative
http://www.ukpol.co.uk/pfi.htm (Labour's Policy, May 1997)
http://www.open.gov.uk/ccta/pfihome.htm (Web-Page)

Proggressive Unioonist Party
http://www.pup.org/ (Web-Page)

Public Appointments Unit
http://www.open.gov.uk/pau/pauhome.htm (Web-Page)

Public Record Office
http://www.pro.gov.uk/ (Web-Page)

Public Trust Office
http://www.publictrust.gov.uk/ (Web-Page)

Quango's
http://www.open.gov.uk/co/publicbo.htm (Government Web-Page)

Queen (See Monarchy)

Queen's Awards for Industry
http://www.queensawards.org.uk/ (Web-Page)

Queens Speech
http://www.number-10.gov.uk/hmspeech/note.html (Notes on the Queen's Speech)
http://www.ukpol.co.uk/qspeech.htm (Text of the 1997 Queen's Speech)

Radio Communications Agency
http://www.open.gov.uk/radiocom/rahome.htm (Web-Page)

Railtrack
http://www.railtrack.co.uk/ (Web-Page)

Railways
http://www.rail-reg.gov.uk/ (Rail Regulator)
http://www.railtrack.co.uk/ (Railtrack)
http://www.rail.co.uk/ (Railways on the Internet)

Rebellion Magazine
http://ourworld.compuserve.com/homepages/rebellion (Web-Page)

Referendum Movement
http://www.euroland.co.uk/ (Web-Page)

Referendum Party
http://www.demon.co.uk/dita/europe/rp/rp_soa.html (Policies)
http://www.demon.co.uk/dita/europe/rp/ (Web-Page)

Regional Parliaments
http://www.smithq.demon.co.uk/#Regional_Parliaments (Web-Page)

Regulators
http://www.ofsted.gov.uk (Education)
http://www.open.gov.uk/offer/offerhm.htm (Electricity)
http://ofreg.nics.gov.uk/ (Electricity and Gas in Northern Ireland)
http://www.ofgas.gov.uk/ (Gas)
http://www.rail-reg.gov.uk (Railways)
http://www.oftel.gov.uk (Telecommunications)
http://www.open.gov.uk/ofwat/index.htm (Water)

Reigate (Council)
http://www.surreycc.gov.uk/rbbc/members.html (Council Information)
http://www.surreycc.gov.uk/rbbc/ (Web-Page)

Republic
http://www.republic.org.uk/ (Web-Page)

Republican Sinn Fein
http://indigo.ie/~saoirse/index.htm (Web-Page)

Restormel (Council)
http://dspace.dial.pipex.com/town/plaza/jf89/ (Web-Page)

Revolutionary Communist Group
http://www.rcgfrfi.easynet.co.uk/ (Web-Page)

Revolutionary Communist Party
http://www.junius.co.uk/ (Web-Page)

Revolutionary Communist Party of Britain
http://www.wwne.demon.co.uk (Web-Page)

Richmond (Council)
http://www.dircon.co.uk/education/ (Education Web-Page)

Rock the Vote
http://www.rockthevote.org.uk/ (Web-Page)

Royal British Legion
http://www.britishlegion.org.uk/ (Web-Page)

Royal institute of International Affairs
http://www.riia.org/ (Web-Page)

Royal Family (Official Page)
http://www.royal.gov.uk/ (Web-Page)

Royal Mint
http://www.royalmint.com/ (Web-Page)

Royal Parks
http://www.open.gov.uk/rp/rphome.htm (Web-Page)

Royal Ulster Constabulary
http://www.ruc.police.uk/ (Web-Page)

Royalist (Web-Page)
http://www.geocities.com/CapitolHill/3115/index.html (US Page)

Rushmoor (Council)
http://www.rushmoor.gov.uk/ (Web-Page)

St, Albans (Council)
http://www.stalbansdc.gov.uk/stalbans/ (Web-Page)

Sandwell (Council)
http://www.open.gov.uk/sandwell/sandmem1.htm (Council Information)
http://www.open.gov.uk/sandwell/newhome.htm (Web-Page)

Satirical Card of the Week
http://www.btinternet.com/~cybercard/weekly.htm (Web-Page)

Save Britains Fish

http://www.savebritishfish.demon.co.uk/ (Web-Page)

School Curriculum And Assessment Authority
http://www.open.gov.uk/scaa/scaahome.htm (Web-Page)

Scientists For Labour
http://www.shef.ac.uk/uni/projects/sfl/agm2.html (1995 Annual Report)
http://www.shef.ac.uk:80/uni/projects/sfl/ (Web-Page)

Scotland (See also under Scottish Office)
http://www.cosla.gov.uk/ (Convention of Scottish Local Authorities)
http://www.alba.org.uk/maps.html (Election Maps)
http://www.alba.org.uk/elections.html (Election Results)
http://www.trp.dundee.ac.uk/data/councils/ncintro.html (New Scottish Councils since April 1996)
http://www.sac.org.uk/ (Scottish Arts Council)
http://www.scotent.co.uk/ (Scottish Enterprise)
http://www.scottishmuseums.org.uk/ (Scottish Museums Council)
http://www.alba.org.uk/ (Scottish Politics Web-Page)
http://www.holiday.scotland.net/ (Scottish Tourist Board)

Scott Report
http://go2.guardian.co.uk/scott/ (Guardian Newspaper's Focus on the Scott Report)
http://www.coi.gov.uk/coi/scott/ (Gvt Press-Pack of Information)
http://www.ukpol.co.uk/shaw1.htm (David Shaw MP's assessment of the Scott Report)
http://www.ukpol.co.uk/shaw2.htm (Ian Lang's House of Commons statement on the Scott Report)
http://www.ukpol.co.uk/shaw3.htm (Opposition comments on Scott Report, compiled by David Shaw, MP.)

Scottish Environmental Protection Agency
http://www.sepa.org.uk/ (Web-Page)

Scottish Enterprise
http://www.scotent.co.uk/ (Web-Page)

Scottish Labour Net Voice
http://www.abel.co.uk/~slabnetv (Web-Page)

Scottish National Party
http://www.cs.stir.ac.uk/~rhh/history.html (History)
http://www.snp.org.uk/ (Web-Page)

Scottish Office
http://www.ed.ac.uk/~riu/GETS/index.html (Education and Training in Scotland)
http://www.the-stationery-office.co.uk/document/scottish/dunreply/dunreply.htm (Gvt's response to Dunblane)
http://www.open.gov.uk/scotoff/scofhom.htm (Web-Page)

Scottish Parliament
http://www.scottish-devolution.org.uk/ (Web-Page)

Scottish Politcs Page

http://www.alba.org.uk/ (Web-Page)

Scottish Socilist Allience
http://wkweb1.cableinet.co.uk/diblake/ (Web-Page)

Sottish Tourist Board
http://www.holiday.scotland.net/ (Web-Page)

Searchlight
http://www.s-light.demon.co.uk/ (Web-Page)

Secret Kingdom
http://www.cc.umist.ac.uk/sk/index.html (Web-Page)

Select Commitees(House of Commons)
http://www.parliament.the-stationery-office.co.uk/pa/cm/cmselect.htm (Reports available on the Internet)

Select Commitees (House of Lords)
http://www.parliament.the-stationery-office.co.uk/pa/ld/ldselinf.htm (Web-Page)

Service First
http://www.servicefirst.gov.uk/

Sevenoaks (Council)
http://www.sevenoaks-uk.com/ (Web-Page)

Shelter
http://www.vois.org.uk/vois-bin/chapter/shelter?3 (Homelessness Costs)
http://www.vois.org.uk/shelter/ (Web-Page)

Shropshire(Council)
http://www.shropshire-cc.gov.uk/council.htm (Council Information)
http://www.shropshire-cc.gov.uk/ (Web-Page)

Single Transferable Vote
http://www.gn.apc.org/ers/stv.htm (Summary from Electoral Reform Society)

Sinn Fein
http://www.ukpol.co.uk/sinn.htm (Information)
http://www.serve.com/rm/sinnfein/ibsub.html (Mitchell Commission Response)
http://www.irlnet.com/sinnfein/ (Web-Page)

Smart Cards
http://www.open.gov.uk/ccta/getsmart.htm CCTA (Web-Page)

Smith Adam
http://www.duke.edu/~atm2/SMITH/ (Wealth of Nations)

Social Exclusion
http://www.open.gov.uk/co/seu/seuhome.htm

Socialist Equality Party
http://dialspace.dial.pipex.com/sep/ (Web-Page)

Socialist Labour Party
http://www.ifley.demon.co.uk/index.html (Web-Page)

Socilist Outlook
http://www.gn.apc.org/labournet/so/index.html (Web-Page)

Socialist Party
http://www.socialistparty.org.uk/ (Socialist Party)

Socilist Party of Great Britain
http://ourworld.compuserve.com/homepages/worldsm/spgb.htm (Web-Page)

Socialist Workers' Party
http://ourworld.compuserve.com/homepages/SWP_Britain/ (Web-Page)
http://www.swp.org.uk/ (Web-Page)

Society Against a Federal Europe
http://www.geocities.com/CapitolHill/Senate/4940/ (Web-Page)

Soctim
http://www.socitm.gov.uk/ (Web-Page)

Solihull (Council)
http://www.open.gov.uk/smbc/index.htm (Web-Page)

Somerset (Council)
http://www.somerset.gov.uk/ (Web-Page)

South Hrefordshire (Council)
http://www.open.gov.uk/hereford/pages/shdc_idx.htm (Council Information)
http://www.open.gov.uk/hereford/pages/shdchome.htm (Web-Page)

Spelthorne (Council)
http://www.surreycc.gov.uk/spelthorne/ (Web-Page)

Sports Council
http://www.english.sports.gov.uk/ (England Web-Page)
http://www.sportscouncil-ni.org.uk/ (Northern Ireland Web-Page)

Staffordshire (Council)
http://www.staffordshire.gov.uk/ (Web-Page)

Statewatch
http://www.poptel.org.uk/statewatch/ (Web-Page)

Stationery Office (Formerly HMSO)
http://www.the-stationery-office.co.uk/ (Web-Page)

Stevenage (Council)
http://www.open.gov.uk/index/filclgov.htm (Web-Page)

Stroud(Council)
http://www.open.gov.uk/strouddc/home-page/home-page.htm (Web-Page)

Student Loans Company

http://www.slc.co.uk/ (Web-Page)

Suffolk (Council)
http://www.suffolkcc.gov.uk/interested_in_us.html (Council Information)
http://www.suffolkcc.gov.uk/ (Web-Page)

Surrey (Council)
http://www.surreycc.gov.uk/scc/members/cllindex.html (Council Information)
http://www.surreycc.gov.uk/scc/ (Web-Pages)

Taking LibertiesTAKING LIBERTIES:
http://www.tim1.demon.co.uk/Articles/articles.html (Articles)
http://www.tim1.demon.co.uk/ (Web-Page)

Tandridge (Council)
http://www.surreyweb.org.uk/tandridgedc/about-tdc.html (Council Information)
http://www.surreyweb.org.uk/tandridgedc/about/publicat.htm (Council Publications)
http://www.surreyweb.org.uk/tandridgedc/ (Web-Page)

Taxation
http://www.ifs.org.uk/research/misc/uktaxsurvey.htm (1997 I.F.S. Guide to the Tax-System)
http://www.ifs.org.uk/ (Institute for Fiscal Studies)
http://www.purple.co.uk/purplet/tax.html (Tax-Net)
http://www.hm-treasury.gov.uk/ (Treasury Web-Page)

Teeacher Training Agency
http://www.teach-tta.gov.uk/ (Web-Page)

Teaching Politics
http://norn.mailbase.ac.uk/lists-p-t/teaching-politics/ (Details of Mailing List)

Teignbridge (Council)
http://dspace.dial.pipex.com/town/terrace/ql68/index.htm (Web-Page)

Test Valley (Council)
http://www.testvalley.gov.uk/testvalley/cons.htm (Conservative Group)
http://www.testvalley.gov.uk/testvalley/alpha.htm (Councillors)
http://www.testvalley.gov.uk/testvalley/lib.htm (Liberal Democrat Group)
http://www.testvalley.gov.uk/ (Web-Page)

Thatcher Margaret
http://www.uoregon.edu/~heroux/2-illiberal.html (British Culture and Thatcherism)
http://reality.sgi.com/employees/keithk/thatcher.html (Moral Foundations of Society-By MT)
http://129.125.8.16/~welling/usa/presidents/reagan/thatcher.html (Thatcher Speech on Reagan)

Third Way
http://www.users.dircon.co.uk/~thirdway/ (Web-Page)

Thomas Paine Society
http://www.hkf.co.uk/TPS/TPS.html (Web-Page)

Thurrock (Council)

171

http://www.open.gov.uk/thurrock/tchome.htm (Web-Page)

Torbay (Council)
http://www.torbay.gov.uk/council/contents.htm (Council Information)
http://www.torbay.gov.uk/ (Web-Page)

Tote
http://www.tote.co.uk/ (Web-Page)

Trade & Industry, Department of
http://www.isi.gov.uk/ (Information Society Initiative)
http://www.dti.gov.uk/Ministers.html (Ministers)
http://www.dti.gov.uk/ost/ (Office of Science and Technology)
http://www.coi.gov.uk/coi/depts/GTI/GTI.html (Press Releases)
http://www.dti.gov.uk/Publications.html (Publications on the Internet)
http://www.dti.gov.uk/Speeches.html (Speeches)
http://www.dti.gov.uk/ (Web-Page)

Trade UK
http://www.tradeuk.com/ (Web-Page)

Trade Union
http://www.gpmu.org.uk/ (Graphical, Paper and Media Union)
http://www.poptel.org.uk/kfat/ (Knitwear and Footwear Union)
http://www.ws.pipex.com/tgwu/ (TGWU Web-Page)
http://www.unison.org.uk/ (Unison Web-Page)

Trade Unions Congress (TUC):
http://www.tuc.org.uk/ (Web-Page)

Transplants From Animals to Humans
http://www.ukpol.co.uk/science.htm (Gvt announces consultation)

Transport
http://www.ukpol.co.uk/min.htm# (tranCabinet Ministers for Transport this Century)
http://www.open.gov.uk/dot/ann_rpt/annrpt.htm (Gvt Spending on Transport)
http://www.open.gov.uk/hiagency/highhome.htm (Highways Agency)
http://www.coi.gov.uk/coi/depts/GDT/GDT.html (Press Releases)
http://www.open.gov.uk/dot/dothome.htm (Web-Page)

Treasury
http://www.bankofengland.co.uk/ (Bank of England)
http://www.euro.gov.uk/ (Euro Official Site)
http://www.hm-treasury.gov.uk/pub/html/minutes.html (Monthly Meetings with the BofE Governor)
http://www.hm-treasury.gov.uk/pub/html/news.html (News Releases)
http://www.hm-treasury.gov.uk/pub/html/top/main.html (Treasury Occasional Papers)
http://www.hm-treasury.gov.uk/ (Web-Page)

Trial by Conspiracy
http://www.coverup.net/ (Web-Page)

Tribune Newspaper

http://www.abel.co.uk/~rost2000/ (tribuneWeb-Page)

Troops Out
http://www.serve.com/tom/misc/who.html (Policies)
http://www.serve.com/tom/ (Web-Page)

Tunisia
http://www.fco.gov.uk/current/1997/jan/09/tunisia.txt (Speech by Jeremy Hanley MP)

Tynedale (Council)
http://www.demon.co.uk/tynedale/ (Web-Page)

UCAS
http://www.ucas.ac.uk/ (Web-Page)

UK Charities
http://www.phon.ucl.ac.uk/home/dave/TOC_H/ (Charities/Web-Page)

UK Citizens On-line Democracy
http://www.democracy.org.uk/ (Web-Page)

UK Elect
http://ourworld.compuserve.com/homepages/timb/ (Web-Page)

UK Independence Party
http://www.CityScape.co.uk/users/fm33/ (Web-Page(Unofficical))
http://www.bath.ac.uk/~ce5krs/ukip.htm (Web-Page(Unofficial))
http://www.btinternet.com/~ukip/ukiphp.htm (Web-Page (Official))

UK Passport Agency
http://www.open.gov.uk/ukpass/ukpass.htm (Web-Page)

UK Politics Newsgroup
http://www.ukpol.co.uk/ukpeo.htm (uk.politics.* people page)

UK Politics On-Line
http://www.global-press.co.uk/politics/index.htm (Web-Page)

Ulster Democratic Party
http://www.udp.org/documents.htm (Documents about Northern Ireland)
http://www.udp.org/ (Web-Page)

Ulster Democratic Unionist Party
http://www.dup.org.uk/ (Web-Page)

Ulster-Scots
http://ourworld.compuserve.com/homepages/w_bradley/ (Heritage Council Newsletter)

Ulster Unionists
http://www.uup.org/text/static/policy.html (Policies)
http://www.uup.org/text/current/c_fire.html (Reaction to the end of the cease-fire)
http://www.uup.org/ (Web-Page)

Unemployment
http://www.unemployment.co.uk/ (Right-to-Work by Sir Ralph Howell)

UNISON
http://www.unison.org.uk/general/survey.html (About UNISON)
http://www.unison.org.uk/ (Web-Page)

United Kingdom Atomic Energy Authority
http://www.ukaea.org.uk/ (Web-Page)

UNited Nations
http://www.amdahl.com/internet/events/un50.html (50th Anniversary of the United Nations)
http://www.un.org/Overview/ (About United Nations)
http://www.yahoo.com/Government/International_Organizations/United_Nations/ (Various Links)
http://www.un.org/ (Web-Page)

United Nations High Commissioer For Refugees
http://www.unhcr.ch/ (Web-Page)

University & College Admissions Service (UCAS)
http://www.ucas.ac.uk/ (Web-Page)

Uttlesford (Council)
http://www.webserve.co.uk/clients/saffire/councils/uttlcoun.html (Web-Page)

Vale of White Horse (Council)
http://www.open.gov.uk/oxcis/html/5025/2FED948.1 (Councillor Information)
http://www.open.gov.uk/oxcis/html/5025/13A1.1 (Web-Page)

Vehicle Inspectorate
http://www.via.gov.uk/ (Web-Page)

Voluntary Organisations Internet Site
http://www.vois.org.uk/ (Web-Page)

Wakefield (Council)
http://www.csv.warwick.ac.uk/~suaba/Politics/Election/Local95/wakefld.res (1995 Local Election Results)
http://www.wakefield.gov.uk/ (Web-Site)

Wales
http://www.plaid-cymru.wales.com/ (Plaid Cymru Web-Page)
http://www.ukpol.co.uk/waters.htm (The Case for a Welsh Assembly, by Lee Waters)
http://www.wales.com/political-party/plaid-cymru/policies/jobs.html (Unemployment in Wales)
http://www.open.gov.uk/woffice/whome.htm (Welsh Assembly)

Wales Tourist Board
http://www.tourism.wales.gov.uk/ (Web-Page)

Walsalll (Council)
http://www.ukpol.co.uk/wall.htm (1996 Local Election Results)

Waltham Forest (Council)
http://www.lbwf.gov.uk/ (Web-Page)

Wandsworth (Council)
http://www.wandsworth.gov.uk/ (Web-Page)

Wansbeck (Council)
http://www.ace.co.uk/CityCard/ (Web-Page)

War Pensions Agency
http://www.dss.gov.uk/wpa/index.htm (Web-Page)

Warrington (Council)
http://www.u-net.com/warrington/home.htm (Web-Page)

Warwick (Council)
http://www.warwickdceh.demon.co.uk/ (Web-Page)

Warwickshire (Council)
http://www.warwickshire.gov.uk/council/ccindex.htm (County Councillors)
http://www.warwickshire.gov.uk/council/dcindex.htm (District Councillors)
http://www.warwickshire.gov.uk/business/tsindex.htm (Warwickshire Trading Standards)
http://www.warwickshire.gov.uk/ (Web-Page)

Waveney (Council)
http://www.waveney.gov.uk/ (Web-Page)

Waverley (Council)
http://www.surreycc.gov.uk/waverleybc/wbchome.html (Web-Page)

Wealden (Council)
http://www.mistral.co.uk:80/wdc/members.htm# (A3Councillors)
http://www.mistral.co.uk:80/wdc/ (Web-Page)

Welfare State
ftp://ftp.demon.co.uk/pub/doc/liberty/LA/dismantl.txt ((Dismantling the Welfare State (Nigel Ashford))

Welsh Development Agency
http://www.wda.co.uk/wda/index.htm (Web-Page)

Welsh Office
http://www.cymru.gov.uk/nhstable/contents.htm (Wales NHS Performance Tables)
http://www.cymru.gov.uk/ (Web-Page)

Welwyn Hatfield (Council)
http://welhat.gov.uk/ (Web-Page)

West Devon (Council)
http://www.wdbc.gov.uk/wdbc/html/whoparsh.html (Councillors)
http://www.wdbc.gov.uk/ (Web-Page)

West Dorset (Council)
http://www.dorset-cc.gov.uk/wddc.htm (Web-Page)

West Dunbartonshire (Council)
http://www.west-dunbarton.gov.uk/ (Web-Page)
http://www.whirlwind.co.uk/ (Web-Page)

West Lothian (Council)
http://www.westlothian.gov.uk/ (Web-Page)

West Mercia Constabulary
http://www.demon.co.uk/westmerc/ (Web-Page)

West Oxfordshire
http://www.ukpol.co.uk/wox.htm (1996 Local Election Results)

West Wiltshire (Council)
http://www.west-wiltshire-dc.gov.uk/ (Web-Page)

Western Isles (Council)
http://www.open.gov.uk/westisle/facts.htm (Information)
http://www.open.gov.uk/westisle/wiichome.htm (Web-Page)

Weynouth (Council)
http://www.weymouth.gov.uk (Web-Page)

Whig Party
http://home.clara.net/gamestheory/whigs.html (Web-Page)

Whirlwind Directory
http://www.whirlwind.co.uk/index.shtml (Latest News)

White Nationalist
http://www.listen.to/counterblastworldwide.org (Web-Page)

Widdecombe, Ann (MP and Former Home Office Minister)
http://www.penlex.org.uk/psn14.html (50th Prison Visit)
http://www.penlex.org.uk/widdecom.html (Biography)
http://burn.ucsd.edu/~archive/riot-l/1996.Jan/0111.html (Denies women chained up when pregnant)

Wigan (Council)
http://www.wiganmbc.gov.uk/Wigan (Web-Page)

Wilson, Harold
http://www.ukpol.co.uk/wilson.htm (Biography)

Winchester (Council)
http://www.winchester.gov.uk/ (Web-Page)

Wirral (Council)
http://www.wirral.gov.uk/ (Web-Page)
http://www.wirral.gov.uk/16-6.htm (Council Committee Functions)

Woking (Council)
http://www.ukpol.co.uk/wok.htm (1996 Local Election Results)
http://www.surreycc.gov.uk/wokingbc/ (Web-Page)

Wolverhampton
http://www.ukpol.co.uk/wolv.htm (1996 Local Election Results)

Worcester (Council)
http://www.open.gov.uk/hereford/pages/wcc/wcc_cc.htm (Councillors)
http://www.open.gov.uk/hereford/pages/wcc/wor_home.htm (Web-Page)

World Bank
http://www.worldbank.org/html/extpb/annrep96/index.htm (1996 Annual Report)
http://www.worldbank.org/html/extdr/thematic.htm (Development)
http://www.worldbank.org/ (Web-Page)

World in Action
http://www.world-in-action.co.uk/ (Web-Page)

Workfare
http://www.coi.gov.uk/coi/depts/GDE/coi2736c.ok (Information from the DofEE)

Worthing (Council)
http://www.ukpol.co.uk/worthing.htm (1996 Local Election Results)
http://www.pavilion.co.uk/wbc/cllrs.htm (Councillors)
http://www.pavilion.co.uk/wbc/ (Web-Page)

Wrekin (Council)
http://www.telford.gov.uk/ (Web-Page)

Wycombe (Council)
http://www.wycombe.gov.uk/ (Web-Page)

Wyre Forest (Council)
http://www.open.gov.uk/hereford/pages/wf_dc/wf_home.htm (Web-Page)

Youth Against the European Union
http://www.geocities.com/CapitolHill/3729/index.html (Web-Page)

Submit - A -Site

Despite my best efforts, and many hours of searching the Internet, there are always some web-sites related to British Politics which I might miss. If you know of any web-sites which you think should be included in this directory - and thus also on the British Politics Internet Page at http://www.ukpol.co.uk/ - then please let me know by e-mailing julian@ukpol.co.uk, or by writing to:

Julian White
Aplex
78-80, Prince of Wales Road
Norwich
NR1 1NJ

This will enable me to keep both this book, and the Internet site, as up-to-date as possible, and together we'll make sure that as many political sites are as accessible as possible. If you note any changes in URLs which any site listed may have made, I'd be grateful to hear about them.